What's Your Problem?

Alex Garcia

ABOUT THE AUTHOR

Jon Yates is a columnist for the *Chicago Tribune*. He grew up in Ames, Iowa, graduated from the University of Iowa, and began his newspaper career in Iowa City. He briefly covered Congressman Sonny Bono for the *Palm Springs Desert Sun*, and was a crime reporter at the Nashville *Tennessean*. He lives in Oak Park, Illinois, with his wife, two kids, and eighty-pound mutt.

What's Your Problem?

Cut through Red Tape,
Challenge the System, and
Get Your Money Back

JON YATES

wm
WILLIAM MORROW
An Imprint of HarperCollins*Publishers*

HarperCollins books may be purchased for educational, business, or sales promotional use. For information please write: Special Markets Department, HarperCollins Publishers, 10 East 53rd Street, New York, NY 10022.

FIRST EDITION

Library of Congress Cataloging-in-Publication Data
  Yates, Jon.
    What's your problem? / Jon Yates. — 1st ed.
      p. cm.
    ISBN 978-0-06-200988-3
    1. Customer services. 2. Consumer complaints. 3. Customer relations. I. Title.
HF5415.5.Y38 2011
381.3'4—dc22

                                      2010053596

12 13 14 15 16 OV/RRD 10 9 8 7 6 5 4 3 2 1

To Trine, Celia, and Quinn

ACKNOWLEDGMENTS

This book could not have been written without a tremendous amount of help from scads of people who have touched my life in myriad ways.

First and foremost, my editor at HarperCollins, Stephanie Meyers, who came up with the idea for this book, then saw it through to completion. Her skillful editing and spot-on suggestions turned my rambling copy into something I'm extremely proud of. I cannot thank her enough.

A million thank-yous to my literary agent, Elyse Cheney, an amazing advocate. Not only is she among the best in the business, she gives a damn good pep talk as well. I'm forever grateful for her guidance and expertise, as well as that of her associate, Hannah Elnan.

Some of the content in this book first appeared in a somewhat different form in the *Chicago Tribune*, where I am a columnist. A tremendous debt of gratitude is owed to my many editors, copyeditors, and photographers who helped make each column stronger. The list is too long to include in its entirety, but includes Gerry Kern, Jane Hirt, George Papajohn, Michael Lev, Greg Stricharchuk, Lorna Lim-Wong, Fauzia Arain, Jane

Fritsch, Mary Jane Grandinetti, Marie Dillon, and former *Tribune* editors Ann Marie Lipinski, Hanke Gratteau, and Steve Kloehn.

I would be completely lost without the help of my partner in crime, Kristin Samuelson. Her amazing work ethic and unfailingly upbeat attitude provide a daily inspiration.

Thank you to Angelynne Amores, who helped me better understand customer service.

A few special mentions, starting with the Chicago Cubs, whose embarrassingly dismal 2010 campaign allowed me to concentrate on the book without the normal distractions of summer. For that, I thank them. Thanks also to the String for its Cubs-fan–like unconditional support.

Finally, words cannot describe how grateful I am to my incredible wife, Trine, a wonder woman if ever there were one. Her influence is evident on every page.

CONTENTS

Contents

What's Your Problem?

INTRODUCTION
The Power Within

Romy Kaminski knew how the system worked. She had spent six years as a benefits coordinator for an insurance broker, helping fellow employees navigate the labyrinthine health care system. She knew the games health insurance companies play, she knew how to speak their language, and she knew how to get results.

Or so she thought.

When she got laid off, Kaminski couldn't afford the $1,300-per-month COBRA payments required to continue with her former employer's health insurance plan. Instead, she signed up for a $225-per-month, no-frills, catastrophe-only plan with a company called Assurant Health.

As luck would have it, catastrophe soon followed. A month after signing up with Assurant, Kaminski collapsed in pain and was rushed to the hospital. An undetected brain aneurysm had burst.

"The guy on the CAT scan machine actually said, 'Oh my God,'" Kaminski remembered. "He said, 'You have tons of bleeding on your brain. I can't believe you're actually talking to me.'"

Doctors performed two surgeries on her brain, and she spent almost two weeks in intensive care. She could never have imagined that her time at the hospital would be the easy part, but by the time she returned from the hospital, her medical bills had beaten her home. She got out her calculator and pecked away frantically, trying to keep up. It made her head hurt all over again.

One bill was for a mind-boggling $162,000. Another was for $84,000, and a third came in at $20,000. Assurant refused to pay any of them. The insurance company ordered all of her medical files, then scoured them to see if she had a preexisting condition—anything that would allow it to deny payment on her claims.

"I absolutely know what's going on behind the scenes," Kaminski said at the time. "They don't want to pay the bill. They're stalling, stalling, stalling. Delay and don't pay; that's their tactic." The former benefits coordinator tried everything she could to convince the company to pony up. It wouldn't budge.

More than six months after her first surgery, Kaminski owed the hospital more than $310,000. Tired of waiting for Assurant to pay, the hospital began sending Kaminski threatening letters, demanding its money immediately. If Assurant didn't come through, she'd be forced to file for medical bankruptcy. Her credit would be ruined. Her savings would be wiped out.

Out of utter desperation, Kaminski wrote to me for help. Less than a week after I called Assurant, the insurance company agreed to pay almost everything.

That's what I do. I'm the Problem Solver.

———

My job is to cajole, threaten, or bully businesses and bureaucracies into doing the right thing. I write a column for the *Chicago Tribune* in which I stick up for society's Davids in their everyday battles against the Goliaths. I am a journalistic enforcer, a heavy, the newspaper's consumer conscience.

With a mere phone call, I can correct erroneous cable bills, convince the city to throw out bogus parking tickets—or help a wayward insurance company see the light. I can get an airline to pay for lost luggage, and ensure the gas company doesn't turn off a poor customer's heat in the middle of winter.

Why am I telling you all of this? It's simple: if I can do this, so can you.

Trust me, I am not your stereotypical thug. Growing up, I was the kid who mouthed the words in chorus, only pretending to sing because I was sure my classmates would laugh at my off-key warbling. I was the second grader who, when my family moved across town, secured a waiver from the school district so I could continue attending my old elementary school. The thought of making new friends petrified me. In college, professors routinely docked me full letter grades for not speaking up in class. I wrote an essay about my shyness for freshman rhetoric class. My professor thought it was a cry for help and asked me to read it in class. I refused.

When I left my home state of Iowa to become a reporter at a newspaper in Palm Springs, I spent my first night in the California desert holed up in a hotel room, sobbing with fear. I kid you not.

Years of solving other people's problems have made me a pro at it, but I'm no tough guy. At 5 feet 7 inches tall, I do not cut an imposing figure or speak with a booming voice. I will never be mistaken for a professional hockey enforcer. I still waver when faced with confrontation and I still dread arguments, even when I know I am right. At dinner parties, I prefer to fade into the background and let my hypersociable wife, Trine, speak for both of us.

My point is not that I am a wimp, although I'd understand if you drew that conclusion. My point is that if I can convince seemingly uncaring bureaucrats and businesspeople to do the right thing, so can you.

Don't get me wrong, I do not believe all corporations are evil, or that all customer service agents are sadistic turds. I do not hold a grudge against government employees, or think they secretly revel in making our lives miserable. Most public servants are fine, upstanding people, and most corporate employees are caring and nice.

But this book is not about them.

This book is about their wicked co-workers who listen but do not hear, make promises they do not keep, and who strive to torment us with each pinprick of lousy customer service.

In my years as the newspaper's Problem Solver, I have learned a few things about the business world. It's true that a large part of my success is thanks to my column. As they say, "never pick a fight with a man who buys ink by the barrel." Businesses and elected officials will almost always correct a mistake at the mere threat of negative publicity.

But my success cannot solely be attributed to my journalistic muscle. Over time, I've discovered that the key to solving your own problems comes down to three basic and universal understandings.

First, all companies, corporations, and utilities are in business for one reason: to make money. To convince them to repair your faulty television or your out-of-whack electric bill, you must first convince them that *not* fixing your problem will cost them more in the long run. When it comes to big business you have to speak its language, and that language is money.

Second, most bureaucrats, bigwigs, and fat cats hate confrontation almost as much as we do. If you push them far enough, they'll cave.

Third, courtesy only gets you so far. Before I realized how the system works, I believed another old adage: "you can catch more flies with honey than you can with vinegar." And sure, if we all treated each other with courtesy and caring, honey would work every time. I always encourage readers to play nice when initially attempting to resolve their problems. Lord knows, we could use a little more civility in this world, and if we can solve a problem with a smile, all the better. But in many cases, the system is designed to chew up and spit out the honey. It only responds to the vinegar, so it's often necessary to store some anger in reserve.

One of my earliest memories growing up in Ames, Iowa, was attending an Iowa State University football game with my dad. My dad, a librarian by trade, is perhaps the most mild-mannered, laid-back person on earth. With shocks of unkempt white hair and a bushy gray mustache, he strikes a remarkable resemblance to Albert Einstein.

He moved the family to Iowa in the late 1960s from Boston after his boss ordered him to fire a fellow employee. My dad, bless his heart, couldn't bring himself to do it. It worried him so much, he gave himself an ulcer. Iowa, he reasoned, had to be better than that.

So the Yates clan settled in Ames, home of the mighty Cyclones, with whom my young self developed an unhealthy obsession. It was 1978, and my dad had purchased great seats for the biggest game of the year, against the Oklahoma Sooners. He wasn't about to let anything, or anyone, spoil it.

We got there early and settled into our ticketed spots on the long bleacher-type bench. As the game went on, more people jammed themselves into our row. By the end of the first quarter, there were so many fans crammed together, I was squeezed clean out of my seat.

Now, I can count on one hand how many times my dad has been truly angry. When completely flustered with someone, he used to call them a "dumb bunny." I'm not making that up. But on that autumn day at Cyclone Stadium in Ames, my dad reached his boiling point. Before the start of the second quarter he stood up, his face red with anger, and lectured our neighboring fans so sternly, *my* face turned crimson.

"Some of you are in this row and should not be, and there is no room for my son to sit," he said, his voice echoing above the din of the crowd. "If you are in the wrong seat, leave NOW!"

Then he stared right down the row with a serious scowl, looking more Clint Eastwood than Stan the librarian. As he brooded, several college students got up . . . and left, embarrassed.

My beloved Cyclones lost the game, 34–6, but the day wasn't a complete loss. For the last two and a half quarters, I enjoyed a comfortably wide berth on the stadium bench. Vinegar, I learned at age eight, works.

And so, as my alter ego Problem Solver, I have often resorted to heaping doses of vinegar, even when it clashes with my gentler instincts. Corporations don't care if you're nice. They'll gladly run you over in their pursuit of another few bucks. To get results, you have to convince them that you won't take no for an answer, and that stringing you along will wind up costing them more in wasted customer service employee hours, or account reviews, or supervisor angst.

If a customer service agent doesn't listen to you, you have to call again. And again. And again. The more time they spend dealing with you, the more it's costing the company. In the rough-and-tumble world of customer service, the sad truth is, sometimes it pays to be a jerk.

But—and here's the part that most people miss—being a jerk will get you only so far. Raising a stink can get you noticed when you call a customer service agent. But you need other tools in your toolbox to get results.

That's what this book is about. It's about understanding what resources are available and learning how to use the media to your advantage. It's about knowing what gets utility companies to act, and what motivates politicians and government officials. It's about understanding how customer service works, and the rules that govern how the agents act. And sometimes, it's about knowing when you need help—and where to go to get it.

———

One of the most heart-wrenching letters I ever received was from a woman named Bella Milman. Two years earlier, Milman had ordered a $2,750 gravestone for her recently deceased father, Mikhail Movirer. It had taken the monument company thirteen months to complete the stone, but that wasn't why she was writing.

After the monument company finally completed the stone, Milman flew from her hometown of Toronto to Chicago to see the finished product. She arrived at the historic North Side cemetery, where her late father rested, and excitedly walked to her father's plot. There she discovered that, instead of "Movirer," the engraver wrote "Wovirer." Her father's name had been misspelled.

Upset, she called the company, which promised to fix the error immediately. Twice it told her the stone had been corrected, and twice she flew from Toronto to Chicago, only to find the marker unchanged.

I called the monument company's owner, who promised to pick up the stone and replace it immediately. Weeks later, the owner sent both me and Milman an e-mail with a picture of the corrected stone. The e-mail, it turned out, was a cruel tease. A month later, the monument company closed and the owner quit answering his phone. The corrected stone was complete, but it hadn't been delivered to the cemetery. Milman had no idea where it was.

She considered giving up. She considered biting the bullet and paying another gravestone company to make a new marker. But Milman had already spent two years fighting for her father's gravestone. She had put in way too much effort to quit.

Without telling me her plan, she began calling other monument companies in Chicago and asking if they knew where the stone was. It took her just three calls to find the warehouse where it sat. After she told the owner her sad story, the man asked her to send a check for delivery. He promised to take the gravestone to her father's gravesite the next day. Milman sent the check immediately. Before it even arrived in Chicago, the man had placed the gravestone at the cemetery.

An elated Milman called me at home on a Saturday. Sobbing, she told me how happy she was to finally have the corrected stone set above her resting father.

"A lot of people told me to just go and pay for another stone," she said. "It took two years of hard work but I would never have given up."

After the column about Milman appeared, I was flooded with e-mails from people who were upset about her situation. The reason it resonated with so many readers was not just the unfortunate circumstances, but the sense that we've all faced similar trials.

Perhaps we haven't been confronted by a double-talking gravestone maker, but we have all dealt with death—and can imagine the added stress of dealing with a belligerent company while we're consumed with grief. Or we've been promised satisfaction by a business that has no intention of following through. Many of us have been duped by con men, scam artists, or simple money-grubbers, folks who see us not as customers but as mere conduits to money.

It isn't just the life-altering events that confound us. It's the little things, too.

Of the hundreds of requests for help I receive each week, a majority of them are what most of us would consider minor. I get scads of complaints from people whose sole frustration is they can't reach a human being at one company or another. Others are upset because they can't find a phone number to call the phone company, or feel a customer service agent has been rude.

In most cases, it is not one thing that has gotten the reader so upset, but an accumulation of small slights that have reached a tipping point. How many times can you calmly call the cable company and get patched through to a language-challenged representative in a faraway country? How often do you have to navigate a seemingly endless string of automated telephone prompts, only to end up leaving a message on an answering machine? How satisfying is it to click through a company's website only to find it offers no answer for your specific problem?

It can be dehumanizing, and, if left unchecked, it takes a toll. I hear the frustration every day. I can't tell you how many letters I have received that start with, "It's not the money involved that upsets me, it's the principle of the thing."

No one likes getting ripped off, no matter how small the thievery.

I once got a letter from a man who had purchased a scoop of ice cream at Baskin Robbins. When he went to pay, the bill was bigger than he had calculated in his head. He scanned the receipt and realized there was an additional charge of twenty-five cents for a sugar cone. His letter was among the angriest I have seen. A simple sugar cone had finally pushed him over the edge.

I can't say I blame him. We've all been nickel-and-dimed half to death.

This book is for those of you who are tired of it. It's about sticking up for yourself and discovering how to navigate an increasingly complicated consumer landscape that will take advantage of you in ways both large and small if you let it. It's about finding your inner toughness, and being creative in the face of a faceless foe.

It's not easy. Every week, I receive hundreds of requests for help. A sizable number are from everyday folks who are too afraid to tackle their problems on their own. If that sounds like you, that's the first thing you'll need to change.

When I first became the Problem Solver, I developed one steadfast rule: I would not help anyone who had not already tried to help him- or herself. The reason is simple. It is not fair to accuse a business of cheating a customer without first giving that business a chance to correct the mistake.

Not all businesses are bad, and most understand that good customer service will make them more money in the long run. It costs most companies far more money to attract a new customer than it does to retain an existing one.

Besides, most customer service call centers are like any rooms full of people. Some of the employees are good, some are bad, and some are simply indifferent. If you call once, it's a roll of the dice whether you'll find a good agent. Call repeatedly, however, and you increase your odds of finding a competent and sympathetic ear. But if you don't call at all, you never stand a chance.

For many months, an elderly woman called me almost weekly, pleading with me to place a call on her behalf to a contractor she was convinced had overcharged her. The man had come to her condo and fixed a broken shower, then charged her more than $1,000.

A handyman in her building said the repair should have cost a fraction of that amount. He convinced her she had been ripped off. She was angry, but also embarrassed—and too shy to call the contractor herself. She was convinced she would just get bullied.

Each time the woman called me I re-explained my rule, and each time she refused to call the contractor. She was simply too scared of confrontation. And so it went on, the elderly woman and I in a hopeless, months' long stalemate while her problem remained unresolved.

Then one day, things changed. Almost giddy, she told me she had finally given up hope that I would call the contractor for her. Like my father had on that fateful day in Cyclone Stadium, she finally reached her breaking point.

With a palpable pride, she told me she had taken matters into her own hands. She had marshaled all her inner strength and called the contractor herself. To her amazement, the man agreed to reduce the bill. Turns out, she had it in her all along.

I've seen it repeatedly in my years solving people's problems. At some point, we must all become our own best advocates.

Romy Kaminski knows that. I spoke to her just moments after she left her neurosurgeon's office where she learned she was, medically speaking, completely recovered. She was ebullient, but still angry about how she had been treated by her insurance company. I asked her what she had learned from the experience. Without missing a beat, she said that perseverance pays.

"Don't give up and don't stop, and if you know you're right, fight," she said. "Just keep fighting until you find the right person to help you."

Kaminski said she hoped to start a new business, a consulting firm to help others who are faced with obstinate health insurance companies. The first thing she'd tell people: it's the sad truth, but sometimes we're simply too nice. When faced with a bill you know you do not owe, be ready to scuffle.

"Don't just give up and start paying," she said. "Don't just think you have to pay for things if you know better."

I couldn't have said it better myself.

REMEMBER:

- Be your own advocate. Don't back down in the face of an uncaring business, and don't part with your hard-earned money easily.
- Don't wait for someone else to help you. Help yourself. You're the only one who can guarantee a full effort.
- To convince a business to respond to your complaint, you must make it clear that not satisfying you will cost the business more money in the long run.
- Play nice. But if playing nice doesn't work, don't be afraid to play nasty. Sometimes, only nasty works.
- Do your research. Figure out how to get to the decision makers, then talk to them directly.
- Don't give up. If you truly believe you're correct, don't take no for an answer. Keep at it until you get what you want—and what you deserve.

1

DIAL H FOR HUMAN BEING
Mastering the Customer Service Call

Arnold Ford helped invent the first computerized phone answering system when he worked for IBM thirty years ago. If he had a time machine, he'd dial up the late '70s, then go back and destroy it.

"It's become a monster," said Ford.

He should know. The Florida resident recently had trouble with his prescription drug program. When he called to sort things out, he found it impossible to reach a human being.

Ford tried calling his insurance company more than twenty times but was continuously thwarted by an endless string of infuriating phone prompts. Each led to a computerized recording instead of a person.

Call it karma.

"It's very frustrating because I know it can work better than this," Ford told me. "We fixed it up so that once you punched zero, a live body would come on."

But the '70s are long gone, and so is many companies' dedication to customer service. Now, businesses use automated phone systems not to help folks like you and me, but to avoid us. As corporations look for new ways to satisfy Wall Street and boost their bottom lines, many have replaced customer service agents with bastardized versions of Ford's creation.

Computerized phone systems are now so prevalent and elaborate that it's virtually impossible to call any major American company and immediately get through to a real-life human being.

Have you ever tried calling AT&T? It's like breaking into Fort Knox. And they're the *phone* company. Um, this is their gig.

I called on a recent Saturday and encountered no less than twelve key prompts before an aggravating computerized voice allowed me to even ask for a customer service agent. By then, it was past 4 p.m. and all the humans had left the AT&T call center.

"Sorry," the computer told me. "This office is currently closed."

How's that for customer service?

The good news is there are ways around this automated phone hell.

The website GetHuman.com has compiled a list of more than eight hundred companies with instructions on how to bypass the labyrinth of keypad prompts and reach a real person. The site's project leader, Walt Tetschner, believes customer service has deteriorated over the years, in large part because of automated phone systems. Tetschner, who also started a sister website called Get2Human.com, said most companies don't intend to treat customers poorly.

"There's no (company) that's going to sit there and say, 'It's our strategy to provide lousy service,'" Tetschner once told me. "I think it's the implementation, how they put it together, that's been so bad."

Both GetHuman.com and Get2Human.com allow users to provide tips, new phone numbers, and rate each business. The websites also list the average hold time for each business, and they often provide multiple suggestions for how to reach a person at each company.

For AT&T, Tetschner's site lists no less than a dozen numbers to call, including one that it promises will connect you directly to a customer service agent (888-387-6270). I tried it the following Monday, and was greeted by a baritone voice that informed me that "all of our customer service representatives are busy answering other customers," but that my call would be answered within five minutes.

I figured I could handle that. After all, there were no key prompts required. And the hold music was a soothing blend of smooth jazz with some oddly calming calypso. It was like being stuck in the world's lamest elevator.

To my utter amazement, after another brief message from the baritone voice (thanking me for my patience and urging me to go online for quicker service), an extremely pleasant customer service agent answered the phone.

"AT&T, this is Andrea," she said. "How can I make this a great day for you?"

I told her she already did, just by answering the phone. Total elapsed time: less than three minutes. If that isn't an all-time AT&T record, I don't know what is.

All automated phone systems are set up differently, and in some cases there will not be a magic phone number like the one I called to get through at AT&T. But Tetschner says there are some tricks that work in most cases.

If a company has outsourced its call center to India, the Philippines, or some other far-flung foreign country and you can't understand what the customer service agent is saying, ask for another agent. If the first agent won't transfer you—or you can't understand the second agent—ask to be transferred to a domestic call center. Tetschner said some companies will actually route the call back to the United States.

That, of course, only works if you get through to a living, breathing person.

If you're dialing in circles and can't break through the computerized system, Tetschner says to first play dead. That's right, the old opossum move. Many automated systems rely on input, so if you don't punch any keys or say anything, the system gets confused and will transfer you to an operator. Some systems also have a default setting for customers with old rotary-dial phones, which it turns out do still exist. After a certain amount of silence, the computer figures you have no keys to push, and it jettisons you to an agent.

"Ignore it," Tetschner said of the menacing phone computer overlord. "Sooner or later you'll get patched through."

If waiting it out doesn't work, hit zero. It might seem like a no-brainer, but it often works. Of course, companies know this, too, and sometimes set their operator default key to another number, often 4 or 7.

If you've hit every number on the phone's keypad and you're

still not getting through, start talking gobbledygook. Sometimes nonsensical words confuse the system and convince the computer you really do need help.

You can also get sneaky. Instead of calling the company's customer service line or repair line, find the number for new customers. Sadly, some businesses make it easier for you to get through if they think you represent a potential sale. Once you get through to a sales operator, ask to be transferred to a customer service agent. The same goes for the company's account collections office. Because it is their job to collect money, the account agents generally don't let customers wait too long before they answer the phone. Once you're in the system, ask to be transferred to customer service.

Even better, search online for the company's name to find direct-dial numbers that are outside the automated system. If you know where the business is located, call information and ask for the number. Often, there are separate numbers for corporate offices.

If you get through to an automated system with an employee directory that asks you to type in the first few letters of the person's name, try keying in the most common last names (764 for Smith, 564 for Johnson, 945 for Williams, 566 for Jones, and so on) until you hit upon one that works. (See the appendix for a list of numbers for the most common surnames). Once you get through to a person there, they might be willing to patch you through directly to a customer service agent—if for no other reason than to get you off their backs! You might also find a more sympathetic ear in the corporate office, where they're not used to hearing customer complaints all day.

In all cases, take notes and ask questions. Some companies impose quotas on their customer service agents, meaning they are expected to handle a predetermined number of calls per day. To reach their quota, the agents will tell you just about anything to get you off the phone. If you feel you are being rushed or your concerns are being glossed over, hang up and call back and speak to another agent.

If you get through to a good customer service agent or a supervisor, ask if they have a direct dial number you can use to reach them again later. Get their names, get their ID numbers, ask what hours they work. A good or caring customer service agent is like gold. Figuring out how to get back in touch with them in the future can be invaluable.

Trust me, not all customer service agents are created equal. I once spent several days shadowing agents in a massive customer call center for the nation's largest cable television provider, Comcast. I had written about Comcast more than a dozen times before, zinging the company as a habitual offender for repeated crimes against customer service. Their public relations woman had assured me Comcast was filled with all manner of good, caring, absolutely normal people, so I figured I'd see the operation in person.

The facility, a gigantic warehouse-like structure the size of an indoor football field, was slathered in earth-tone paint and bathed in fluorescent light. On almost every wall, there were inspirational posters with encouraging phrases to remind the call takers that, despite the drab surroundings and nonstop barrage of complaining customers, everything in the Comcast universe was just great. I was told the call center was designed to be comforting, but the ultrabright artificial light made me feel like I was stepping onto a casino floor—or the world's largest X-ray machine. At least none of these folks was going to fall asleep on the job.

Hundreds of cubicles splayed out along the call center's main floor, creating a maze of customer service agents. There was a soft buzz as they chattered away on telephone headsets.

I walked through, my head spinning. I was face-to-face with the enemy.

Well, maybe "enemy" is a bit strong. As one customer service agent told me, "We are your mother, your sister, your family. We do care." She meant it, too.

But as the day wore on, I realized that as with any family, there are good apples and bad ones. And as I listened in on customer service calls that day, it became apparent that getting ahold of one of the good apples is a complete crapshoot.

Some customer service agents were prompt, courteous, and efficient. Others were not. One woman called to complain about her Comcast e-mail account and was patched through to an agent who was downright rude. The customer did the right thing: she hung up on him.

In fact, not only did she hang up, but she immediately called back to another customer service agent to complain. Good move. The next customer service agent was so appalled at her colleague's behavior that she gave the woman a credit of a month's worth of service toward her bill.

The lesson? Never settle for bad customer service.

GETTING WHAT YOU WANT WHEN CALLING CUSTOMER SERVICE

- Try, try again. If the first agent isn't helpful, call back, and continue calling until you get an agent you're comfortable with. Don't be intimidated by the process or by some thickheaded, uncaring agent. You're paying his or her paycheck—you deserve quality care.
- Take your time. When you find a customer service agent you're comfortable with, don't rush. Have all your facts and papers in front of you, both to ensure you can answer the agent's questions, and to ensure you bring up all of your concerns.

  Before calling a company, I often take a piece of paper and write down all of my points and some of the key facts in a small outline or cheat sheet. I check off the points as I talk to make sure I don't miss anything. There's nothing worse than finally getting through to a competent call taker, only to have to call back again because you forgot something.
- Get it in writing. Always, always ask for promises to be made in writing. I can't tell you how many people have written to me to say a customer service agent promised to erase an erroneous charge, only to find no changes had been made to his or her bill. In some cases, the company will argue "there's nothing in our computers that shows you were told you will get a month of service for free," or "our customer service agents aren't authorized to give you such a deal."

If you ask for the agreed-upon changes to be written down and sent to you, either in the mail or by e-mail, you have rock-solid proof.

- Read the terms and conditions. This is particularly important when it comes to contracts agreed to over the phone. One of the most frequent complaints I receive is that a cell phone company or satellite television provider has locked a customer in to a multiyear contract that includes a hefty cancellation fee, sometimes in the hundreds of dollars.

The contracts, which can run for two years or more, often automatically renew if you don't opt out when the initial time frame ends. The contracts can also renew if you ask for a change in service, such as adding a channel to your television lineup, or if you change your cell phone for a newer model.

In many cases, you don't even realize you've signed a long-term contract because you've agreed to it over the phone—not in writing. By agreeing to a long-term contract with a termination fee, you've essentially ceded your most important consumer tool: the threat of quitting and signing up with a competitor.

You've given the company no incentive to treat you well. Without the fear of losing you as a customer, the company can respond slowly to your complaints—or not respond at all—and you have little recourse.

My advice? Never agree to a contract that includes a large cancellation fee, and never agree to something over the phone without first seeing the terms and conditions in writing.

- Be wary of "limited time offers." Customer service agents often pressure you to sign up now by offering special deals that they say are only available at that moment. In almost every case, that same deal will be available in a few days or a few weeks, after you have had a chance to read and review the terms of the contract. Trust me, there's always another deal out there.

Think of cable and telephone companies like drug dealers. They'll offer you anything under the sun to get you in the door and hooked. Three free months of HBO? No problem. A $100 gift certificate to your favorite restaurant? It's yours. Unlimited calling for just $19.99 a month? You bet.

But remember, all of these offers are merely short-term payoffs. Once you've agreed to the contract, the companies have you under the lion's paw. After the three months of HBO runs out, you have to pay for it. And $100 worth of food isn't much compared to what you'll be paying over the life of a two-year cable contract. If you agree to pay $59.99 a month, that's a whopping $1,440 over the course of the contract. And that unlimited calling plan for $19.99? After the special low introductory rate ends, you're responsible for the full price of the plan, which is almost certainly significantly more.

In other words, don't let a sales agent sweet-talk you. Always know what you're getting into. Take your time and shop around. The first deal you're offered is often not the best.

LOOK BEFORE YOU LEAP

As I was writing this book, I looked at several so-called "incredible" offers from various cable television, Internet, and phone companies, all of whom desperately wanted my business. While the deals sounded great, most of them carry a commitment to ongoing payments that can total hundreds or thousands of dollars.

Below is a look at the true cost of a few of the deals—not including taxes, fees, and upgrades.

- Comcast had a "limited-time offer" of digital cable for just $29.99 a month. The special rate ended after six months, and beyond that, regular rates applied, starting at $56 a month. After a year, I would have paid $515.94. The true monthly cost of this $29.99 deal? $42.99 per month.
- DIRECTV offered more than 150 channels at $29.99 per month for twelve months. When I read the fine print, however, I saw I had to submit an online "rebate" form, which could take up to eight weeks to process. I also had to commit to two years of service. After the first year, the price increased to $58.99. If I canceled early, I'd be charged a fee of $20 per month for each remaining months. The total cost: $1,067 over two years, or $44.46 per month. If I canceled after the first year, the total was a mere $599.88, or $49.99 per month.
- AT&T wireless offered a "free" Samsung Strive cell phone, which it touted as a $169.99 value. But to get the phone, I had to sign a two-year service agreement, with the cheapest plan costing $39.99 per month. I also had to sign up for a

text-messaging contract for at least $20 a month, and agree to one "additional service," the most affordable being roadside assistance for $2.99 a month. The grand total after two years: $1,511.52 ($68.98/month) for the cheapest option, $2,231.52 ($92.98/month) for unlimited calling.

- Do your homework. At the Comcast customer call center, each agent had access to a computer program that allowed them to type in a customer's address and *zing!* pull up all of the competitors that offered service in that neighborhood. On their computer screens, the agents could view the competitor's plans, rates, and special offers. To get or retain a customer, the agents are trained to sweeten the deal and stay competitive.
- It's information that can benefit you as well. Do some research before you call. Know what the competition is offering in your area. If AT&T offers cheaper service than Comcast, let the agent know you've looked around. Often, he or she will do what it takes to keep you. There's nothing better than letting large companies fight for your business. It's one of the few instances where you, the customer, have control. Don't relinquish it easily.
- Review your conversation. Before you hang up, ask the customer service agent to review everything you've talked about. Make sure the agent understood what you've asked for or agreed to, and that it's in the company's computer system. Ask again for a confirmation e-mail or letter and note the agent's name and ID number. Don't leave anything to chance. Because chances are, if you do, it will come back to haunt you.

Throughout all this, don't ever forget: you're the one in control. You've got what companies want: your hard-earned money. Don't part with it easily or foolishly. In almost every circumstance, there is competition for your business. Use that power wisely.

REMEMBER:

* If you can't get through to a human being when calling customer service, try staying silent, speaking gobbledygook, or pressing numbers.
* If you still can't get through, look up the number for the corporate offices or financial offices.
* Once you get through, get the customer service agent's name and ID number, and take copious notes on your call.
* Never settle for a bad customer service agent. Call again—and again—until you get a good one.
* Be wary of long-term contracts and cancellation fees.
* Ask for all promises to be sent to you in writing.
* Don't be pressured into making decisions immediately. Take your time.
* Use your power as a consumer wisely. You have the money, so you're the one in control. Make companies fight over your business.
* Remember that enticing offers usually mean higher costs in the future.

2

POISONED PEN
Writing a Successful Complaint Letter

Sometimes, a mere phone call won't do. Sometimes a customer service agent simply won't listen. Or worse yet, the agent will listen but do nothing to help you. Sometimes, you can do everything right, you can have all your ducks in a row and all the facts on your side, but you still find yourself banging your head against the concrete wall of customer service.

It can make you want to chuck it all and give up. I've been there. But there's always another option. Just ask Dennis Petrille, who learned long ago that filing a complaint with a company's rank and file is often an exercise in futility. Sometimes, you have to move all the way to the top of the corporate food chain.

Petrille's journey through bureaucratic hell began shortly after his elderly aunt, Antoinette, downsized from her home to a more manageable apartment. Before she moved, Antoinette called AT&T and asked to have her phone service stopped. She paid for basic service through her moving day, and asked for long-distance charges to be forwarded to her new address.

No bill arrived from AT&T, but six months later, she received a letter from a collection agency telling her she owed

$140.60. Petrille, who has power of attorney for his aunt, called AT&T and was told she owed $54.40 for long-distance charges before she moved. Petrille verified the calls and agreed to pay that amount.

He asked about the remaining $86.20 and was told it was for five months of basic service—after she had canceled her service and moved. Petrille spoke with an AT&T customer service agent, but she wouldn't budge. Nothing he said could convince the phone company to erase the erroneous charges.

So he sat down at his computer and started typing. He addressed the letter to Randall L. Stephenson, chairman and CEO of AT&T.

"Dear Mr. Stephenson," he began. "I am writing on behalf of my 86-year-old aunt regarding some mistaken billing by AT&T."

Over the next page and a half, Petrille detailed what had happened to his aunt and the effort he had gone through to get it corrected. He calmly laid out the facts, with dates and names and charges. He told the company's chairman that he had tried to get the matter resolved through the company's customer service line, but was unable. He didn't ask for anything he wasn't entitled to. He simply wanted Stephenson to make things right.

"What I ask is that my aunt be allowed to pay AT&T the $54.40 and the remainder be dropped," he wrote. "Also, that [the collections agency] be informed to bow out. Your assistance seems to be the only way out of this morass."

He signed it, "Sincerely, Dennis Petrille."

A few days later, someone from AT&T called him. The company agreed to drop the charges.

"Kind of renews one's faith in corporate America," Petrille told me.

Well, not quite. But it did restore my faith in the power of the written word—and the power of bypassing the often-ineffectual bottom rungs of a corporate ladder by going straight to the decision makers at the top.

When I asked how Petrille had decided to go this route, it turned out that he had done this before, with amazing results. When he bought a new toilet that had some minor defects, he tried calling the manufacturer, who was not particularly responsive. So he wrote a letter to John Menard, owner and founder of the Menards Home Improvement Store chain where Petrille had purchased the commode. A short time later, Menard—which, thankfully, understood how critical a functioning toilet was—delivered a brand new toilet.

"The world has become harsher," Petrille told me. "There was a time when you could get good customer service. I don't know if it's part of this reduction of costs companies are going through, but they've gone over the edge. It's definitely harder to get satisfaction."

Over the years, Petrille said, he's written at least a dozen complaint letters to corporate CEOs.

"I'd say 90 percent of them have been effective," he said. "A lot of CEOs are sympathetic if you write them."

Penning a well-written letter to corporate bigwigs can quickly cut through layers of bureaucracy and get your problem directly into the hands of the decision makers. Even the most well-intentioned customer service agents often feel like their hands are tied in certain circumstances. They are given guidelines and rules to follow and if your issue falls outside their parameters, they are often unwilling or unable to help.

In some cases, customer service agents aren't given the power to erase charges, make permanent changes to accounts, or amend the terms of a contract. I once wrote a column for the *Chicago Tribune* about a woman who had flown to a conference in Salt Lake City. Her husband was supposed to follow her there on a flight three days later for a short vacation.

The day before he was scheduled to fly, the husband died unexpectedly. Distraught, the woman asked for help from the desk supervisor at her hotel in Salt Lake City. The supervisor, a kind woman named Ashley Perry, called American Airlines and rescheduled the woman's flight home, but the American Airlines customer service agent refused to refund money for the late husband's flights.

In fact, the airline's customer service agent was so rude, Perry sat down the next day and wrote an angry letter to the airline's president. She detailed the circumstances and wrote how disappointed she was in American's response.

"I was just upset because, being a supervisor, you have to make decisions and know when there are extenuating circumstances," Perry told me. "I was like, how can you act like that?"

A few weeks after Perry vented in her letter to American Airlines' executives, the widow received a letter from the airline. It offered to refund her the cost of her late husband's flight.

WRITING LETTERS THAT WORK

What makes a successful complaint letter?

It starts with a little research. Before writing a word, go to the Internet and look up the company's CEO and board members. If you can't find them through a search engine, look on the company's website. Usually executives and board members can be found in the "investor relations" area of the company's site. Sometimes, the investor relations website is separate from the website that's designed for consumers, so if you can't find a link on the company's webpage, search for it separately.

If you still can't find the executives' names, search for press releases or news articles about the company. You can also call the customer service line and simply ask for the names and the address of the corporate headquarters.

Make a list of the top dogs—executives in the corporate offices. Double check to make sure you have their names spelled correctly and their addresses and titles right.

CHECK IT TWICE

How important is it to be accurate with the executive's name? Back in college, the editor of my college newspaper was named Loren Keller. Some readers couldn't seem to grasp that Loren could be a man's name, so they wrote letters to "Ms. Loren Keller," or "Lauren Keller," or simply "Ms. Keller."

"My name got spelled countless numbers of ways," he told

me later. "I would collect all of those misspelled labels and stick them on the bulletin board."

When the novelty wore off, he simply threw them away.

"Those were letters I was certainly a lot less likely to pay attention to," Keller said. If there's any doubt about an executive's gender, do yourself a favor and leave out the "Mr." or "Ms."

When you write your letter, make several copies and send one each to everyone on the list. At the bottom, note everyone you've sent the letter to by putting a short "CC'd." In many cases, if the executives know you've sent it to others in the company as well, someone on the list will feel compelled to respond, if only to cover his or her butt in the presence of a higher up.

It also never hurts to send copies to some local media and put their names on the "CC'd" list as well. Knowing a newspaper or television station might be sniffing around sometimes provides the extra incentive a company needs to act. No one wants bad publicity, and savvy companies know that by responding quickly to your letter, they might be able to avoid an unflattering article or television news story. I receive e-mails almost daily from readers who say the mere threat of contacting me was enough to convince a business owner to resolve their problem. Yes, sometimes it's just that easy.

Now, don't get me wrong. I don't think the executives will actually read your letter. Perhaps a few will. But odds are, the CEO's assistant will read it, and often that's enough. Companies like to look responsive, especially at the highest levels, so generally someone will respond to your complaint. Usually, it's someone who can actually help you.

Once you have your list of recipients in order, you can get down to the business of writing. Always include your name and account number or identification number—anything you think would be helpful for the company to quickly look up your account. Remember, even if your name is Joey Joe-Joe Junior Shabadoo or some other highly uncommon name, the world is a pretty big place. Odds are there is at least someone else out there who shares your name, and he or she might also be a customer of this company (you'd be amazed how many Jon Yateses there are, even with the slightly unconventional spelling of my first name). Make sure the company knows exactly who it's dealing with.

As I've said before, vinegar works, so it's okay to have an edge to the letter. Let them know you're upset. But keep things civil and by all means, avoid profanity or threatening language. The impact of the printed word is blunt and permanent. Writing offensive language or insults can immediately alienate the reader and make him or her less sympathetic to your cause.

When writing, try to be concise. Corporations receive truckloads of mail every day. The longer the letter, the less likely an executive—or the executive's assistant—will read the whole thing.

Clearly detail your complaint, along with dates and names and numbers. Again, make it clear you are upset, disappointed, and willing to never use the company again. But make your case through the facts, and make sure the facts are right.

If you have documentation (a bill, a contract, a receipt, a written promise from a customer service agent, etc.), include a copy with your letter. Highlight the pertinent passages to make it easier for a busy executive to follow along. Do not include documents that are not necessary. If you send an entire package of paperwork, it can be overwhelming and confusing. Keep it to the most important few pages. And by all means, send copies of the documents, not the originals. If you send the originals, you'll likely never see them again—and a key piece of evidence you need to prove your case will no longer be available.

Succinctly state what you want done, and don't get greedy. If you want an erroneous charge erased, write the exact amount in question—don't ask for an entire year of free service. Remember, you're in the right and you're entitled to compensation—but only what you're owed. If you leave it to the company to decide how to make things right, they might decide to offer you less, or determine it's too much work to deal with you and move on.

Do not ramble. Stay focused on the task at hand. If you've gone over two pages, you've gone too far. Pare your letter down to the bare essentials. Think of it as a prizefight. Take a few quick, hard jabs. Don't linger in the ring until you, and everyone else, runs out of gas. In most cases, short and concise packs the greatest wallop.

At the end of the letter, say that you've always enjoyed being a customer and that you'd like to continue the relationship, but only if the issue gets resolved. Put your name, address, phone number, cell phone number, e-mail address, and any other contact information at the end. Make it as easy as possible for the company to contact you if it has questions. If you only put your address, it can take weeks for a response letter to arrive. If you then have to respond to the company's letter, the entire episode can drag on for months.

When you're done writing the letter, proofread it for errors. Better yet, have a friend or family member look it over. Misspelled words and names can sink an otherwise perfect letter, giving the reader the impression you didn't care enough to get it right. The same goes for factual mistakes.

"You can't play the crybaby," Petrille said. "You have to have a logical set of facts."

And go straight to the top.

"You often waste your time trying to get anything done at a lower level," he said.

The man knows what he's talking about. Just look at his sparkling new commode.

REMEMBER:

* When writing a letter to a company's headquarters, send copies to more than one executive or board member. Also send a copy to local media.
* Include your account number and other identifying information.
* Be direct and edgy but not profane, insulting, or threatening.
* State your complaint succinctly and accurately.
* State exactly what you want done.
* Don't get greedy. Ask only for what you're entitled to.
* Include any documents that prove you are right—but don't put in too many.
* Never send original documents. Always send copies.
* Be concise.
* Proofread.

3

BRAVE NEW WORLD
Harnessing the Power of the Internet

Okay, I know what some of you are thinking. Writing a letter might be effective, but it's not exactly the fastest solution. Sending your complaint through the postal service takes time. They don't call it snail mail for nothing. There are, as you're probably well aware, more immediate options. Yep, the Internet. Companies can still run, but they can't hide anymore.

Just go online and search for "T-Mobile Sucks." In a fraction of a second, 2.4 million websites pop up in which someone is complaining about the wireless phone company. There are more than three hundred Facebook pages devoted to the topic, and almost two hundred YouTube videos in which folks profess their displeasure with the company.

How does this help you? Like I said, companies aren't exactly keen on negative publicity. Most have whole armies of public relations employees devoted to smoothing over the company's public image. While they can't combat every complaint—especially if there are 2.4 million of them—corporations try to soften the message in areas they can control.

How does it work? Let's use Sasha Jackson of Sayreville, New Jersey, as an example. When the nineteen-year-old was having problems with her T-Mobile phone, she did what any tech-savvy teenager would do: she tweeted about it.

Jackson logged on to her Twitter account and angrily typed, "so sick of this phone, about to hop on the blackberry. But before I do I'm going to call @tmobile." She was smart about it. Before tweeting, she researched T-Mobile and found that it had its own Twitter account. She included the company's account name in her complaint. Better yet, she threatened to go to another service provider if she didn't get satisfaction.

She didn't even need to send the tweet to T-Mobile. Simply broadcasting it to Twitter was enough to get the cellular phone giant's attention. A T-Mobile employee who scans the Twitterverse for mentions of the company saw Jackson's tweet and responded in less than thirty minutes.

As social media websites like Twitter and Facebook grow, companies like T-Mobile are hopping on board, hoping to use the forum as marketing tools. But to appeal to many Internet users, companies can't just broadcast information; they must also look responsive. Many businesses maintain their own Twitter and Facebook accounts, using them to send out good news—and react to bad publicity.

Some companies assign employees to cruise social media sites and respond to posts mentioning the company's name. In Jackson's case, she didn't even have to contact T-Mobile to get a response. All she had to do was mention the cell phone company, and it came to her.

"I was bored at home and my phone was really aggravating me, so I thought, let's tweet about T-Mobile," Jackson told me. "I really didn't think they would respond."

Did she get her issues resolved? Well, not immediately. While social-media websites can get you a quick response, they also have limitations. Twitter limits messages to 140 characters at a time—not exactly ideal for describing a complicated issue. And while posting a complaint publicly has its advantages (companies often respond because they know other Internet users might be watching), there are downsides as well. You have to make sure you do not post personal information or account numbers on a website for all to see. That's like giving an identity thief the keys to your house. Use social-networking sites to start a conversation, but once personal information becomes involved, switch to a controlled forum, such as e-mail or the phone.

In Jackson's case, her Twitter complaint got her in the customer service door. It took additional calls and a visit to a nearby T-Mobile store to get the glitches on her phone fixed, but it all started with that one little tweet.

Using social media and other websites can also be a useful way to resolve time-sensitive issues when customer service isn't coming through.

Take world-renowned quilter Ricky Tims.

Tims was ushered through customs when he changed planes at O'Hare International Airport on his way home to Colorado from a seminar in Dubai. He was given his bags and asked to recheck them before boarding his flight to Colorado. Tims made it to the Colorado Springs airport on time. A suitcase containing one of his most prized possessions, a $40,000 quilt he made, titled "Bohemian Rhapsody," did not. In a panic, Tims began calling United's customer service hotline.

"I made ten or eleven calls to India," Tims said. "I couldn't get anyone to tell me anything about the bag."

On many of the phone calls, he felt like he was shouting into an abyss.

"During my third or fourth phone call they said 'we're working on finding your Samsonite bag with Cuban cigars in it," Tims recalled.

His bag was a cigar-free American Tourister.

After two days of calling, Tims had about had it with the airline. United employees repeatedly promised to call him back with information, but none did. So he got creative.

He posted his story on Facebook, Twitter, and on a blog he writes. He embarked on an all-out assault, using every means at his disposal to get the word out. His goal was to get United's attention one way or another. It worked.

After reading Tims's Internet posts, members of the quilting community rallied behind him. Two of them even e-mailed me at the *Chicago Tribune*, begging me to use my powers as the Problem Solver to step in and make some calls on Tims's behalf. I would have done it, too, but it turned out I was too late. Tims had done just fine on his own.

In little more than one day, he created such an intense Internet buzz that an executive at United Airlines took notice. On day three of Bohemian Rhapsody Luggagegate, Tims was awakened at 6:30 a.m. by a call from a United employee. She told him she had been assigned to his case by her boss, who wanted the issue resolved immediately. She said she was willing to do anything in her power to get his bag returned to him.

Tims said he spoke to the woman five more times that day.

By mid-morning, the airline had located the missing suitcase in a storage room at O'Hare. It was placed on the next flight to Colorado Springs and delivered to Tims's door by late afternoon.

He attributes the airline's turnaround to the power of the Internet. He said the key in his case was not merely posting his story far and wide, but acting quickly and not waiting for United to act on its own. If he had waited for the airline to find his bag through its regular process, he's convinced he would never have received it. He firmly believes his quilt would have been lost forever in the vast and mysterious luggage underworld at O'Hare.

What can we learn from Tims's story? Well, for one thing, don't mess with quilters. And, of course, use the Internet to your advantage.

There are ancillary benefits to airing your complaints about a company on the Web. Even if a company does not respond, your story immediately becomes public and searchable by anyone else with an Internet connection. Consumers looking for a new cell phone provider might cruise the Internet and stumble across Jackson's tweets about T-Mobile. Her experience might convince them to take their business elsewhere. It might also provide valuable insights to other T-Mobile customers facing similar problems who are looking for tips on how to resolve their issues. We're all in this together—the more knowledge we share about companies, the more empowered we as consumers become.

As we saw with T-Mobile, there is no shortage of information about businesses available on the web. If you have a specific problem with a company or product, try to find if someone else has already written about it. A quick search of your local Better Business Bureau or state attorney's office websites can help you determine if others have filed complaints. Sometimes, the details provided in these complaints can help guide you to a solution.

The ever-growing body of Internet complaints can help you sift out the good companies from the bad when you're looking to buy something or sign up for a service. Before handing over your hard-earned cash to a company, you should at the very least do a search on the company's name. You might be surprised what you find.

If the company maintains a Facebook page, peruse the posts to see what others have written. Some companies remove negative comments. Others do not. If you find a page with negative comments, read them to see how the company responds. Only a handful of employees monitor social-media websites in most cases, and like any other form of customer service, some are better than others.

Because interactions on websites are available for public consumption, it often does not take long to identify the good online customer service agents, who usually identify themselves by first name. If you plan to post a complaint, don't do so in anger. Take a few moments to compose your thoughts. Remember, when you click SEND, your post is sent immediately, so make sure it's accurate, succinct, and proofread before you're ready to post it. In most cases, you don't have to include every detail in your initial post. You simply want to get the company's attention.

When Kyleen Robertson ran into problems with the laptop computer she bought from the Best Buy in Wentzville, Missouri, she took it back and was promised a refund. Initially, she was told the $656.39 would appear on her credit card immediately. When it didn't show up, she called customer service and was told it could take days. Days later, she was told it could take weeks or perhaps months.

To Robertson, it sounded like Best Buy was merely trying to push her off and make the issue go away. So Robertson "decided to take more aggressive measures."

She went on Best Buy's Facebook fan page and wrote simply that she had experienced terrible customer service. Almost immediately, a customer service agent responded, asking for more details. So Robertson typed them in. She ended the post by saying she was a member of Best Buy's Premier Club, but not for long.

"Never again will I spend one penny in your stores," she wrote. "I am sick to my stomach over this and not once has anyone sincerely apologized for the crap I have had to deal with."

Minutes later, Justin, a Best Buy "community connector," wrote back.

"Oh my goodness! I'm quite dismayed while reading your poor experience through purchasing/returning your Toshiba computer," he said. "I can only imagine how irritated you must be to go through such lengths to get a refund for your computer."

He didn't stop there.

"Regrettably, I cannot wipe away this experience from your memory," Justin wrote. "However, I will surely document your views expressed to be internally addressed within Best Buy. Also, I realize that you expressed your stance in never wanting to do any future business with us, but is there anything that we can do to save it? You are a valued customer of ours and we welcome your feedback."

To Robertson, it sounded well and good, but all she really wanted was her money back. Over the next several days, Best Buy representatives promised repeatedly to issue the refund, but it never came. Tired of waiting, Robertson went a step further. She found e-mail addresses for Best Buy executives and sent off an e-mail to about two dozen of them. She included her original posting on the company's Facebook page, along with Justin's response. She also wrote a short summary of all she had been through.

"It was just straightforward and to the point," she said.

The next morning, her refund was processed.

DIGGING UP ADDRESSES

How did Robertson find the executives' e-mail addresses? Consumer advocacy website Consumerist.com has compiled a list of addresses for some companies (which is where Robertson found Best Buy's information), and other consumer websites keep similar lists for specific industries, such as airline watchdog site Elliott.org, which includes e-mail addresses for ex-

11/15/2014

Item(s) Checked Out

TITLE   What's your problem? :
BARCODE   33029095599601
DUE DATE   **12-06-14**

Thank you for visiting the library!

Sacramento Public Library

www.saclibrary.org

Terminal #   216

ecutives at Delta, American Airlines, U.S. Airways, and many other carriers.

In most cases, a simple web search including the company's name and the phrase "executive e-mails" will lead you to a website that includes top management's contact information. If that doesn't work, you can sometimes find executives' e-mail addresses on the companies' websites included in the management team's bios. In some cases, the addresses are included in press releases found in the company's Internet press rooms.

As a last resort, as long as you know the executives' names, you can fall back on trying out the two most basic e-mail formulas used by companies: firstname.lastname@company.com and firstinitiallastname@company.com.

What did Robertson learn in her tussle with Best Buy? Like Tims, she said it pays to complain using several different platforms. Her posts on Facebook helped get the company's attention. Her e-mails to the top twenty-five people in Best Buy's corporate headquarters helped seal the deal.

REMEMBER:

* If you have a problem with a company, conduct an Internet search to see if others have had similar issues—and if they have tips for resolution.
* A quick search can also help you decide whether to

patronize the business or organization in the first place.

* Complaining via Facebook, Twitter, or other social media websites can get you a fast response.

* Follow up your social-media complaint with e-mails, calls, or letters. Strike while the coals are hot.

* Rally all the Web resources at your disposal. Putting your story out there often puts pressure on a company to respond.

* Never post personal information or account numbers on public websites or message boards.

* If you find a customer service agent who is helpful on the Internet, take down his or her name, contact information, and work schedule. You never know when you'll need him or her again.

4

A ROYAL PAIN
Getting the Health Insurance You've Paid For

It was five minutes before 5 p.m. on Bob Deaver's 50th birthday when the doorbell rang. When he opened the door, a delivery-man handed him a certified letter. Deaver assumed it was a card from a friend who was working in Iraq. He smiled at the gesture, then opened the envelope. He began reading the enclosed letter and about had a heart attack.

It wasn't a greeting card. It was a missive from his health insurance company. The letter informed him that his policy had been rescinded—taken away for allegedly lying about his medical history several months earlier.

In one fell swoop, his health care safety net was gone. The revocation didn't just affect him. The insurance company also revoked coverage for his wife and three kids, and it did so retroactively. Enclosed was a check for the past year's worth of premiums, along with a note saying he was now responsible for paying back all his previous claims.

"At that point, I was kind of in shock," Deaver told me. "I wasn't sure if I should go upstairs and lie in bed and not move for two days or what. I had no idea this was coming."

He was still dazed when his wife led him to the car and

drove him to a nearby restaurant where his friends and family had gathered for a surprise party.

"I walked through the door. I was walking like a zombie. They yelled, 'Surprise!' My jaw was down by my ankles, and people said 'from the look on your face, you were really surprised.' But it was really still the shock from the letter. I was just kind of saying to myself, 'If I eat something, I'm going to throw up.'"

He soldiered through, trying his best to enjoy the evening. But the next morning, Deaver got right down to business. His goal was simple: to find out why his insurance company had unceremoniously dropped him, and what he could do to get reinstated.

Of all the industries consumers complain about, few are more important—or more confusing—than the health care industry. As the Problem Solver, I'm inundated with complaints about health insurance companies. The process is fraught with paperwork errors, coding mistakes, unclear policies, and bizarre accounting procedures. I've seen claims get denied for seemingly no reason and policies revoked for the smallest of errors.

Have you ever tried to make heads or tails out of an insurance company's explanation of benefits? It can trip up even the savviest consumer. There's a reason the federal government took aim at the health insurance industry in a series of sweeping reforms that began in 2010.

As we saw earlier with the story of Romy Kaminski, a single decision by your insurance company can cause months of intense stress or perhaps financial ruin. Even less dramatic examples, like a denied claim, can have a huge impact on your checkbook and your psyche.

Dealing with health insurance companies is frequently frustrating and intimidating, but you don't have to get wiped out by an unfair decision. The key is to know the facts, and to use them to fight tooth and nail for the coverage you deserve (and paid for).

"You have to know your rights," said Deaver, who spent almost three decades dealing with insurance companies as a dentist before learning the system more intimately with his surprise birthday letter. "Knowledge is power. I had the knowledge that just because they say it's so doesn't make it so."

Before tackling any health insurance problem, you need to understand your policy. If you work for a large company, there's a good chance your health plan is self-funded or self-insured by your employer. That means your coverage is paid for by a combination of your premiums and your employer's contributions. In such a case, the insurance company is merely a third-party administrator, approving or denying claims based on guidelines set by your bosses.

In self-insured plans, also known as employer-sponsored group plans, it is your employer's money that is at stake in claim decisions, not the insurance company's. So if the insurance company unfairly denies a claim, your best bet is generally to complain to your employer's benefits coordinator, a move I learned years ago, when my first child, Celia, was born.

At the time, my wife and I had separate health insurance policies. We both worked for the same newspaper, and two individual policies cost less than a family plan. So our benefits coordinator advised us to wait until our daughter was born, then switch to family coverage.

The hospital was just a few blocks from the newspaper, so a few days after my daughter was born, I walked to my office and filled out the forms to ensure that my new bundle of joy was covered.

Months later, we began getting bills from my wife's obstetrician. At first, the bills were small, about $400 or so. We refused to pay on principle. We had already written a check for the co-pay, and the rest of the birth was supposed to be covered. My wife was told by her doctors not to worry; it would all get taken care of.

Weeks later, bigger bills began to arrive, including one for a mind-boggling $14,000. The insurance company, CIGNA, had denied coverage for the birth.

My wife called CIGNA dozens of times, and received a laundry list of reasons why the claims had been rejected. No two explanations were ever the same. After months of frustration, a customer service agent told my wife the root of the problem: CIGNA's record showed my wife had canceled her coverage on the day Celia was born.

Of course, the insurance company's explanation made no sense. We didn't switch our policy until days after the birth. No matter how you sliced it, my wife was covered that day. But try telling that to a customer service agent whose computer screen tells a different story.

My wife made more calls, and more bills arrived at our home. Already stressed from caring for a colicky newborn, my wife was beginning to lose what was left of her patience.

We didn't have an extra $14,000 lying around—we were knee deep in diapers, wipes, and pacifiers. And for those of you who haven't dealt with a colicky baby, let me tell you, it is even less fun than a stubborn insurance company.

One morning, the stress of the situation finally broke my ever-steady wife. She opened a letter from a collection agency and melted down. She handed me the baby, walked straight to the bathroom, and locked herself in. Sleep-deprived and tired of fighting CIGNA, she began to weep.

I knew I had to do something.

I did a little asking around and discovered our newspaper's health plan was a so-called "self-insured" plan. That meant it was totally funded by the paper; CIGNA merely administered the policy. The insurance company decided which claims should be covered based on guidelines the paper established.

When push came to shove, it was the paper's decision, not CIGNA's, whether to pay a claim. I figured we could keep pounding our heads against the wall dealing with the insurance company, or we could go straight to the folks who called the shots.

I marched into my newspaper's benefits office and explained the situation to the benefits coordinator.

Perhaps it was my disheveled, hadn't-slept-in-days appearance. Or maybe it was the fact that I looked on the verge of going postal. Whatever the reason, she listened to my horror story—and was appalled. That day, the newspaper instructed CIGNA to process the claims.

Several days after that, the claims were paid, and I learned the valuable lesson that solving problems takes some research.

If I had continued talking to the folks at CIGNA, I'd still owe that $14,000 today and my wife might still be locked in the bathroom.

Self-insured plans are overseen by the U.S. Department of Labor, which sets the rules for how a claim must be filed—and how a denial can be appealed. The rules are spelled out in the federal Employee Retirement Income Security Act, or ERISA.

If you work for a smaller company or buy your insurance on your own, you likely have an individual insurance plan. In such plans, it is the insurance company's money at stake. Such plans are generally overseen by your state's insurance department.

Either way, it's important that you know the details of your plan. While it can be mind-numbingly boring, it's imperative that you read your insurance policy thoroughly and understand which procedures are covered and which are not—and it's best to do this before you actually need to use the information.

Pay particular attention to procedures that are excluded, which often include oral surgery and elective procedures. Don't leave it up to your doctor or the doctor's office to check if a procedure is covered. Look it up yourself. I can't begin to count how many e-mails I've received from readers who were stuck with staggering medical bills after they unknowingly underwent an uncovered procedure. Yes, this adds a little time on the front end, but it can save you months of grief—and thousands of dollars—later on.

If you're having difficulty understanding your policy, call your insurance provider and ask questions. If your policy is employer-funded, you can ask someone in your benefits department for guidance. Do not be intimidated by medical jargon or bizarre terminology. If you don't understand a term or phrase, it's always better to get it explained than to run into unexpected problems in the future.

Once you know your policy's rules and who controls the purse strings, you are ready to fight an unjust decision. In some cases, it's as simple as filing an appeal to a denied claim. In Deaver's dental office, challenging a denied claim is a matter of routine.

"A week does not go by where I don't have to send a letter to an insurance company appealing a claim," he said. "It's almost like there's a department where they deny everything that's marginal and they count on your not fighting it."

His advice? Always fight it, and never give up.

When his coverage was rescinded, Deaver pulled out all the stops. He immediately called his insurance provider and asked why his coverage had been revoked. A customer service agent told him he had failed to disclose a preexisting condition. The insurance company cited a form filled out by his doctor at a checkup months earlier that indicated he was bipolar.

Deaver, who is not bipolar, requested the form from his doctor's office and quickly realized the mistake. His doctor had marked a box on a checklist of conditions and the top of the checkmark accidentally continued through the box indicating "bipolar."

Still, his insurance company wouldn't budge. So Deaver got busy. Like Ricky Tims in the previous chapter, Deaver marshaled all available resources. He called his congressman to complain. He filed a complaint with his state department of insurance. He called his insurance company repeatedly.

"It seems like if they get enough heat from enough sources they almost feel as if they have to spend more time and money to fight it than to just pay it," Deaver said. "It's almost like there's a point of diminishing returns where they realize that it will cost them less."

As I've said before, it pays to be a pain in the butt. It took Deaver three weeks of considerable effort, but he got his insurance coverage reinstated.

"I think they just throw this out there and expect a lot of people to just give up or forget about it," he said. "This is my story and it's probably pretty typical."

WHAT SHOULD YOU DO IF A CLAIM IS DENIED?

Often, it's simply a matter of speaking up. Always read your bills carefully and make sure claims are paid in accordance with your plan. If your co-pay for a doctor's office visit is $20 but the bill says you owe $50, don't just pay it—call the insurance company and your doctor and ask what went wrong. In most cases, the two entities will work together to remove the extra $30 from your bill. But if you're not reading your bills—and if you don't complain—you'll wind up paying the extra charges every time.

What if the insurance company flat out refuses to pay a claim? Call the doctor's office immediately. Most physicians' offices have an employee dedicated to keeping track of insurance claims. Doctors know that it's in their best interest to get a claim paid because they're more likely to receive payment from a deep-pocketed insurance company than they are from a patient, especially if the bill is an expensive one.

The doctor's office can often smooth things over and get the insurance company to pay. You'd be shocked how often a claim is denied based on a simple coding error—a number is transposed or a letter mistyped. A doctor's office or hospital can identify such mistakes quickly and resubmit the claim.

If that doesn't work, it's time to file an appeal. If your insurance policy is employer-sponsored, federal law gives you 180 days from receipt of the denial notice to file an appeal. That might sound like a lot of time, but it can slip away quickly. Don't procrastinate. As time ticks away, so does your motivation. Get your ducks in a row and respond to the denial as quickly as you can.

Before filing an appeal, make sure you have all of your paperwork in order. Make copies of any documents that might help you argue your case, such as pertinent medical files. Depending on the nature of the denial, you might want to search the Internet for medical studies that could help convince the insurance company that the procedure in question was justified.

Ask your doctor to write a letter on your behalf. If you're like me and have minimal knowledge about how the human body works, your doctor will better understand the medical jargon and be able to cite specific studies that can help prove your point. The more ammunition you have, the better.

Copy the portion of your policy that states your procedure should be covered. Highlight as necessary. There's no better way to fight an unjust claim denial than to use the insurance company's own words against it.

When you speak to a customer service agent from your insurance company, take detailed notes. Write down dates, times, and the names or identification numbers of all customer service agents you speak to.

Ask the insurance company for documentation to support their denial, and talk with your doctor or doctor's office for advice on how to refute it.

When filing an appeal, make sure to include your name and the identification number from your insurance membership ID card. Include the date or dates of medical service, and the doctor's name. Include a copy of the bill and all related medical records. Write a detailed letter explaining why you think the claim should be paid. While emotional appeals might work in trying to get your cable bill corrected, they have little effect in a medical claim appeal.

"It's a very emotional time, but you have to keep your composure," Deaver said. "The message gets lost if you're screaming."

Most insurance companies respond to appeals within thirty or sixty days. If you're facing a life-or-death situation, you can ask for an expedited appeal, which requires an insurance company to respond much faster, usually within seventy-two hours.

If your appeal is denied, most insurance companies allow you to appeal again. For self-insured (i.e., employer-sponsored) plans, this will be your final opportunity for an internal appeal. For private plans, if you are denied a second time, you will generally have a third level of appeal. By then, of course, you're probably exhausted and frustrated. No matter how you slice it, fighting an insurance company is no fun. But don't get discouraged, and don't let the insurance company wear down your resolve.

I t's important to not just walk away," said Ron Pollack, executive director of Families USA, a national organization for health care consumers. "It requires tenacity, and often people don't have the ability to be tenacious because they're dealing with their own health problems."

If you're not physically or emotionally up for the fight, ask a friend or family member to help. You can also consult a non-profit agency like the Patient Advocate Foundation, which provides counseling and mediation for patients facing chronic, life-threatening, and debilitating illnesses.

Erin Moaratty, chief of external communications for PAF, said her organization has a 98 percent success rate when fighting a denied claim on a patient's behalf. The key? Understanding the process.

"It's really like an investigation," she said. "If you're following your contract like you're supposed to be, there's always an opportunity to win your appeal."

Throughout the process, stay in touch with your doctor's office so the billing staff knows you're not simply ignoring the bill. There are few things more frustrating than spending countless hours battling your insurance company, just to find out that while you were fighting, your doctor put your unpaid bill through to a collection agency.

Even if your appeal to the insurance company is denied a third time, you still have options. As mentioned earlier, if your plan is self-funded, you can ask your company's benefits co-ordinator to consider your case. If that doesn't work, you can consult your regional Employee Benefits Security Administration office, which in some circumstances will intervene on your behalf. (More information on how to find your local office is available on p. 49 in the appendix.)

If you have an individual or nonemployer-sponsored group health plan, some states allow for an external review of disputed claims on private health insurance policies. Such a review is available only after you've exhausted all of your appeals with the insurance company.

To pursue an external review, you must usually file a dispute with your state's insurance commission. Some insurance commissions will advocate on your behalf if they view the insurance company's actions as an obvious violation of your rights. Check out the National Association of Insurance Commissioners' website at NAIC.org for a full list of state insurance departments.

Under provisions of the massive health care act President Obama signed into law in 2010, all health insurance plans will be forced to develop a straightforward and independent appeals process. The new law made it illegal for insurance companies to rescind coverage after people get sick, or to deny coverage to children based on preexisting conditions. In 2014 the law will expand, making it illegal to deny coverage to adults with preexisting conditions as well.

Of course, the new provisions came a bit late for Deaver. In his case, a simple misreading of a routine medical form caused him more grief than most people experience in a lifetime. It wasn't easy, and it certainly wasn't pleasant, but he was able to get his insurance fully restored. His advice? If you're right, keep complaining until you get results.

"Just write, talk, and call," he said. "Eventually someone will listen."

REMEMBER:

* Study your health insurance policy carefully. Know exactly what is covered and what isn't, and what your co-pays and deductibles are.
* Before any major medical procedure, make sure it is covered by your health plan. Call the insurance company yourself—don't rely on your doctor's office to make the required inquiry.
* Read your bills and explanation of benefits statements carefully to make sure your claims were properly paid.
* If you feel a claim is unjustly denied or you were improperly charged, call the insurance company immediately.
* If your initial call does not get results, file an appeal.
* Seek help from your doctor or your doctor's office, which can advocate on your behalf.
* Make sure your appeal is filed quickly, and that it includes all pertinent information. Be sure to point out the portion of your policy where it says the procedure is covered.

* If you have a self-insured or employer-sponsored plan, ask your employer's benefits coordinator to intervene on your behalf.
* If you exhaust all of your plan's appeals and still think you're right, contact the appropriate governmental authority.
* For self-insured plans, contact your regional Employee Benefits Security Administration office.
* For private and group plans that are not employer sponsored, contact your state's department of insurance.
* Never procrastinate. The longer you wait, the less chance you have of getting your dispute resolved.

5

THE UNFRIENDLY SKIES
Troubleshooting Your Travels

Once upon a time, the airlines treated passengers like kings and queens. On cross-country journeys, flight attendants served meals on plates made of china, with real cutlery and actual glassware. Ticket agents handed out vouchers for even the slightest inconvenience. If your flight was delayed, they'd give you a meal ticket. If you got bumped from a flight, they'd set you up in a hotel. Heck, at the slightest turbulence, an airline employee would gleefully hand you a drink voucher.

Now it seems like you need a fifth of vodka just to deal with a two-hour trip.

Flights are routinely oversold, bags get lost or destroyed, check-in lines can stretch for hours, and by the time you're through security, you've removed more clothes than a soft-core porn star. And that's *before* the TSA pat down.

You want a drink ticket for your troubles? Fat chance. A simple meal voucher? Do they even print those anymore? And a *hotel* voucher? You're dreaming. You're just lucky if you get from point A to point B without a major meltdown (by you or the airline).

How bad has it gotten? In its 2009 survey, the American Customer Satisfaction Index found that passengers rated airlines below virtually all other industries, including telephone service providers, banks, the U.S. Postal Service and the Social Security Administration. ACSI cited "high fuel price volatility, indifferent service, labor problems, congested airports, and financial challenges" as reasons for customers' dissatisfaction.

So what happened? And more important, what can we do about it? Terry Trippler, who runs the passenger help website rulestoknow.com, believes the salad days of airline travel are long gone. But that doesn't mean you have to put up with bad service.

"The airlines really spoiled us in terms of how they treated us," said Trippler, who worked as a ticket agent for Northwest Airlines in 1968, also known as the good old days. Back then he'd walk around with a stack of ten vouchers, ready to issue freebies at a moment's notice.

"The idea was to take care of the customers and make them happy," he said. "The industry was regulated then so everyone had the same fares. So to compete, we had to provide better service. Now the fares are basically the same, but they sure as hell aren't out to help the customers."

Like any other industry, the airlines abide by a simple set of rules. Knowing them can mean the difference between winning your battle and joining the ever-growing Disgruntled Fliers Club.

A few years ago, I received a letter from a woman named Shannon Tadel, who had been tapped on the shoulder while waiting to board a plane in Syracuse. A United Airlines employee wanted to speak to her privately.

He pulled her aside, away from the other waiting passengers, and began to tell her a seemingly impossible story. Turns out, a baggage handler had placed Tadel's suitcase too close to the exhaust of a belt loader on the tarmac. The results were not pretty. An airline employee had turned on the belt loader and, voilà! Luggage flambé. Her suitcase was engulfed in flames.

Dumbfounded, Tadel got on the plane and found her seat. Moments later, the pilot beckoned her to the cockpit and pointed out the window to her bag, which was still smoldering on the ground. He told her that, obviously, he could not allow the bag on the airplane. She agreed.

An airline employee escorted her onto the tarmac and helped her fish out a bottle of medicine, then returned her to her seat in economy. She called her brother on her cell phone.

"They just lit my bag on fire," she told him, barely able to believe she was uttering the words. After she hung up, she sat there incredulous until a flight attendant came back and offered her an open seat in first class.

For many months, that was the last kind act United afforded her.

When Tadel arrived at baggage claim after her flight, she found her well-done bag had been replaced by a much smaller piece of luggage containing only a fraction of her clothing. Surprised that anything had survived, she opened the new bag and was overpowered by the smell of charred clothing. A pair of jeans was pockmarked with burn holes. A crumpled blouse was streaked with black stains. Splotches of black soot covered her turtleneck sweater.

She was instructed to make a list of all that was damaged or missing. Dutifully, Tadel dug through the bag and made a list.

"The stench was so bad that I asked to go outside with it, but was told it wouldn't be possible," she said.

Tadel filed a claim, asking for $3,000 in compensation. She thought she had an open-and-shut case, considering that it looked like someone had doused her clothing in gasoline and then lit a match. The truth wasn't far off.

A few weeks after she filed her claim, United called to ask her for her burnt clothing back. The airline needed to study the evidence. Tadel packed it up and sent it in—but not until after she painstakingly photographed the damaged clothes.

Smart move.

Weeks after she sent in her burnt clothing, United still hadn't responded, so she called again. And again. At one point, United even tried to dry-clean the clothes, apparently thinking a good cleaning would magically regenerate the charred cotton fibers. (Needless to say, it didn't work.)

In the end, after months of effort, United finally cut Tadel a check for $3,000, enough to replenish her wardrobe and get a new suitcase. How'd she do it? She became a royal pain in United's backside. She pestered the airline and refused to stop calling when it simply sat on her claim. She jumped through all the airline's hoops, and kept checking on the status of her file.

"I'm not really a pushy person in general, but I had to get pushy to get it done," Tadel told me. "I know that's how the system works. You have to push through any kind of claims yourself."

Good advice. Odds are, you'll need it someday. If you fly even occasionally, chances are you will eventually encounter some sort of similar frustration. Maybe not torched clothing, but perhaps a missing bag.

According to the federal government's Bureau of Transportation Statistics, roughly four suitcases per thousand passengers are mishandled. That might not seem like a lot, but experts say the numbers can be deceiving because they are based on customer complaints. Some bags that are only temporarily delayed go unreported, and passengers who lose small items or suffer minor luggage damage might not file a complaint.

"If you're a frequent flier, it's not a matter of if something will go wrong, but when," said Todd Curtis, founder and director of AirSafe.com. "My bottom line is every time you check a bag, plan on something going wrong."

That doesn't mean you're helpless. First off, take measures to reduce your risk of luggage problems. Never, ever, place valuables or important documents in a checked bag. That means no jewelry, no medicine, no passports—nothing you absolutely need, and certainly nothing that might prove irresistibly attractive to a baggage handler or security worker who makes little more than a basic living wage.

Curtis suggests keeping all valuables in your carry-on bags, including electronics like iPods and computers. But with many airlines now charging fees for checked bags, overhead bins are filling up quickly. So even if you arrive at the airport not intending to check a bag, you might board a plane to find the overhead bins already stuffed full.

What happens next? A flight attendant plucks your bag from your hand and slips you a claim ticket. Suddenly, your perfectly packed carry-on has become an oh-so-tempting piece of checked luggage, loaded down with everything you hold near and dear.

So Curtis suggests going one step further by placing a small bag within your carry-on bag that contains the items you absolutely cannot lose. That way, if you are forced to check your suitcase at the last moment, you can simply pull out the smaller bag as the flight attendant whisks the larger one away.

If you know you will have to check a bag and you have a camera or photo-equipped cell phone handy, lay out everything you are planning to pack on your floor or bed and snap a quick picture. It might not make for award-winning photography, but if your bag winds up missing or something is stolen, at least you have proof of what you lost.

While most missing bags show up within forty-eight hours, some remain missing forever. In such cases, you must submit a missing-luggage form to your airline, including detailed information about your bag and what was in it (along with the photo if you have one). If your bag arrives but some of the contents have been stolen, you should file a complaint not just with the airline, but also with the Transportation Security Administration, which provides the airport screeners. That way you have two swipes at the aviation apple. With any luck, at least one of them will pay off.

How quickly the airline responds—and how much they reimburse you—varies on the airline and the circumstances, but there are rules. The federal government caps airlines' liability at $3,300 per bag (as if you needed yet another reason not to put that $10,000 diamond necklace in your checked suitcase).

Airlines are also supposed to reimburse you for basic necessities if your bag is lost or delayed. This generally covers items like toiletries and anything else you might need to get by until the bag is located. Some airlines will give you money to cover essentials right on the spot. It never hurts to ask.

For international flights, the liability limit was set at the Montreal Convention, a meeting of representatives from countries across the globe. The limit varies based on the strength of the dollar. As of this writing, the limit was $1,730 per bag.

At the end of the day, how much you're compensated depends on how well you document your losses, how quickly you file your claim, and how persistent you are in pursuing your complaint.

United Airlines didn't just hand Tadel $3,000. It took her some effort—and her case was as solid as they come.

Of course, lost bags are only the tip of the iceberg when it comes to airline frustrations. Deteriorating customer service, combined with a string of highly publicized tarmac delays, led the Department of Transportation to pass a new set of rules to protect customers that went into effect in April 2010. Besides limiting the amount of time an airplane can sit on the tarmac, the rules require airlines to respond "in a timely and substantive fashion to consumer complaints."

It sounds all warm and fuzzy to me. But from the sheer volume of e-mails I receive each week from enraged passengers, I get the feeling the airlines aren't exactly playing ball.

To be fair, it is now easier than ever to complain about the airline industry, and passengers have taken advantage. The Department of Transportation has an entire division devoted to complaints about airline service called the Aviation Consumer

Protection Division. It allows passengers to file complaints by phone twenty-four hours a day at 202-366-2220. You can also mail your complaint or fill out a form on the department's website, www.airconsumer.dot.gov. How's that for convenience?

Filing a complaint with the DOT is never a bad idea. For one thing, all complaints are entered into the department's computerized monitoring system, which helps identify industry-wide problems, as well as problems with specific airlines. Better yet, you can review the department's report on the complaints, allowing you to compare the records of different airlines. It's a pretty good research tool that can help you determine which airlines to support—and which ones to avoid.

The DOT website has links that spell out the rules airlines must abide by, including the guidelines for lost or damaged luggage, as well as tips on travel scams and how to interpret your "contract of carriage"—the mind-numbingly boring fine print that comes with your ticket.

The website also contains the federal government's rules for delayed or canceled flights. But before you get too excited (and I know you were), let's first dispense with the bad news. There are no federal rules or protections for passengers if a flight is delayed or canceled due to weather, air traffic, or mechanical failures. In other words, the airlines don't *have* to compensate you in the event of an ice storm, delays caused by other planes, or if some odd doohickey on your airplane fails to perform correctly in a preflight check. And if an airline doesn't have to compensate you, in all likelihood, it won't.

If your flight is delayed or canceled, you should immediately try to figure out why. If it's a mechanical problem, which is the airline's fault, you might be able to convince a customer service agent to provide you with a meal voucher or a free hotel stay. But as we've discussed earlier, such freebies have generally flown the way of the dodo bird.

GETTING BUMPED

There is one piece of good news. If you're lucky enough to have a ticket to an oversold flight, there's always the possibility you'll get "bumped." How, you ask, can this be good for you? Well, in a few ways. Unlike delayed or canceled flights, over-booked flights are regulated by the government, giving you a chance to cash in on an otherwise miserable experience.

On overbooked flights, the government requires airlines to first ask for volunteers to give up their seats and take another flight. If you're not in a hurry and have some flexibility, such an opportunity can become your golden ticket.

"This is the time to negotiate," said Trippler. "This is the time to get the best deal you can for yourself."

Meals, money, free airline tickets—it's all on the table. But if you do agree to get bumped, make sure you know exactly what you're getting. Ask which subsequent flight the airline is going to put you on. Are they putting you on standby or do you have a reserved seat? If they give you a free round-trip ticket to sweeten the pot, ask if there are restrictions. Never agree to anything without knowing exactly what you're going to get.

If no one steps forward to volunteer, you might get bumped involuntarily. If the airline bumps you from an overbooked flight against your will, it must compensate you based on strict federal guidelines. If the airline can get you on another plane that will arrive at your final destination within an hour of your originally scheduled arrival, the airline does not have to give you a penny. (Sorry.) If the delay is between an hour and two hours, the airline must pay you an amount equal to the one-way fare to your destination, up to $400. And if the flight they bump you to includes a delay of more than two hours, the airline must pay twice the cost of a one-way fare—up to $800. In all cases, the airline must also allow you to keep your original ticket for use on another flight. Not too shabby, eh?

In fact, at the time of this writing, the Obama administration was pushing for even stricter rules that would push the top payment for a bumped flight up to $1,300, and would give bumped passengers twenty-four hours to cancel reservations without paying a penalty. Check the Department of Transportation's website for the most up-to-date rules, including all recent changes.

The cold hard truth about the airlines is that they're pretty much like any other industry out there. You just have to know your rights, and invoke them when necessary.

Many of the principles that we've covered in previous chapters apply here, too. First, if a flight attendant, ticket agent, or customer service worker promises you something, ask for it in writing. The odds aren't exactly great that Edna in ticketing will believe you when you tell her Joe at the customer service desk promised a $300 refund. With written confirmation, however, Edna has no choice but to honor it.

Second, complain on the spot. As we discussed earlier, try-ing to get a human being on the phone at most companies can be about as pleasant as banging your head against a concrete wall. With the airlines, imagine the wall is adorned with metal spikes. And the spikes have been heated with the fiery exhaust of a belt loader. By complaining on the spot, you're guaranteed to speak face-to-face with a living, breathing, and hopefully compassionate human being.

When my wife and I traveled to Europe many years (and two children) ago, we spent the entire vacation snapping hundreds of photos. In the warm glow of traveling abroad, we were convinced that each snapshot was a photographic masterpiece, a cherished keepsake that we would hand down through generations of Yateses. Our children would page through our photo albums and marvel at the fact that we actually stood next to a concrete statue of Stalin in Budapest, or that I drank from a ridiculously (and, in hindsight, embarrassingly) large beer stein in Munich.

Okay, we were young. But at the time, those photos meant more to us than the vacation itself. So when we changed planes in Amsterdam on our way home, I nearly had a heart attack in the terminal when I realized I had left my camera bag, with all of our precious film, on our previous plane.

I pleaded with the gate agent to let me back on to get it, but she insisted security rules forbade it. None of the airline personnel were willing to go back and look. On the verge of a nervous breakdown, I nearly stormed the gate myself, before my wife prevailed and talked some sense into me.

Crestfallen, I boarded our connecting flight. Our memo-ries were gone forever. Then I experienced an airport miracle.

A flight attendant from the previous flight had gone back on the plane and retrieved my camera bag. She came aboard my connecting flight and handed it to me in my seat, just before takeoff. Turns out, my embarrassing little display had worked.

Was I lucky? Perhaps. But by pleading my case, repeatedly and loudly in person, I was able to convince at least one airline employee to help. And that's all it takes.

WHEN VACATIONS GO AWRY

All Ken Choi wanted was a family vacation—a road trip to Myrtle Beach with a few sightseeing stops along the way.

He had the whole thing planned perfectly, right down to the hotels. To save money, he booked through Expedia, including an $89-a-night room at the Econo Lodge in Cave City, Kentucky, just a few miles from Mammoth Cave National Park.

By the time he rolled his minivan into the motel parking lot, all he wanted to do was unload the kids and go to sleep, but when he opened the door to his room, Choi realized that wasn't going to happen.

It was the smell that hit him first, a dank, musty odor that seemed to burst from the room. He looked up and saw wallpaper hanging loose from the wall, pushpins keeping it in place.

Upon closer inspection, he saw dark, repulsive splotches. Mold.

"We couldn't stay there," Choi told me later. "My kids are allergic to mold."

Still tired from the drive, Choi loaded his family back into his minivan and drove to the nearest available motel room, thirty miles away in Bowling Green. Then he set about the difficult task of getting reimbursed for his spore-infested room.

With the advent of discount travel websites, booking hotel rooms, airline tickets, and rental cars has never been easier— or cheaper. But the lower cost comes at a price. Now, when something goes wrong with a reservation, travelers often find themselves fighting a two-front battle, dealing with not only the hotel, airline, or rental car company, but with the discount website that provided the deal.

In Choi's case, he immediately complained to an employee at the motel's front counter, but the employee said she could do nothing. Because he had booked through Expedia, Expedia had paid for the room. To get a refund, he would have to ask the discount travel website, the motel employee said.

Expedia refused. It told Choi it had described the room as "two-star" quality. Apparently, that description included the possibility of mold.

What should he have done?

Mark Britton, a former executive at Expedia, said it's imperative to read the terms and conditions of the Internet travel company before you make a purchase. Hotwire, for example, takes your money when you book, not when you travel, making it more difficult to get a refund later.

When you leave for your trip, print out all of your documentation and keep copies with you at all times. Never put the printouts in your checked bags.

If your flight is canceled or your hotel room is substandard, your first complaint should always be lodged with the airline or hotel.

"It's always more efficient to go directly to the travel provider," Britton said. "The travel provider is the one who can most easily rectify the situation."

Daniel Edward Craig, an author who spent more than twenty years working for hotels, said travelers who experience problems in a hotel or motel should complain immediately to the front desk, and ask for the property's manager. Generally, the manager has more power to make decisions, such as issuing a refund or moving you to another room.

When you complain, always have a suggested remedy in mind. If the manager offers you a free breakfast but you're on a company expense account that pays your meals anyway, that's not superhelpful. Ask for exactly what you want.

If you're still not satisfied with the hotel's response, you can always call the corporate headquarters. Even more powerful, Craig said, is the threat of posting a negative review online on a website such as TripAdvisor.

"When a guest has a beef with a hotel, they post it online, and it's very painful for a hotel to have a scathing review," Craig said. "It's hard on morale, not to mention reputation."

In most cases, hotel managers will fix a problem to avoid a negative online review.

In general, hotels are more inclined to help or upgrade travelers who booked directly with the hotel as opposed to customers who booked through a discount website, like Hotels.com or Travelocity. Because the discount sites take a cut of the proceeds, hotels make less money off of those bookings. Hotels also prefer to help customers they consider loyal. Buying a room directly from the hotel costs more, but shows the hotel you are more inclined to return.

If you're traveling overseas, check the hotel reviews carefully before booking. In many countries, hotel standards are lower than in the United States, so online reviews can help prepare you for what you might encounter.

For your flight overseas, try to get all of your connecting flights on the same airline. The more airlines involved, the harder it is to resolve a problem if something goes wrong. Some discount travel sites now offer to cut costs by offering flights on one airline going one way and another airline coming back. If possible, avoid such scenarios.

Britton said fliers should also avoid paper tickets when possible. Airlines treat paper tickets like money, so if something goes wrong, they often require you to send in the paper tickets in order to get a refund, significantly slowing the process. Refunds on electronic tickets can be processed with a few clicks of a mouse.

Of course, it helps to have the truth—and the proof—on your side.

In Choi's case, he kept every relevant document, including pictures of the offending mold. He forwarded his file to me, and I forwarded it to Expedia's corporate headquarters.

Faced with an avalanche of evidence (and some fairly disgusting photos), Expedia caved. Within days, the online travel agency had negotiated with Econo Lodge to get Choi a full refund. It also offered him a $100 gift certificate toward his next trip.

REMEMBER:

* Know the rules. There are federal limits to how much you can be reimbursed if an airline loses or damages your luggage. Study the regulations on the federal Department of Transportation's website.
* Be smart when packing. Never put valuables in a checked bag.
* If possible, take a picture of your belongings before you pack them.
* If your luggage hasn't appeared within forty-eight hours, file a missing-luggage form with both the airline and the TSA.
* Know the limitations. For domestic flights, you can be reimbursed for up to $3,300 per lost bag. On international flights, the limit is roughly half that.
* If you're bumped from an overcrowded flight, the airline must pay you compensation.
* If your flight is oversold and you have time to volunteer for a later flight, work out a deal with the airline. Ask for the sky and take the best deal you can get. Make sure to get all the details.
* Whenever possible, complain in person at the airport.
* Ask for all promises in writing.
* If you have a particularly bad airline experience, file a complaint not just with the airline, but also with the DOT.

6

TOUGH LITTLE GUYS
Avoiding Contractor Cons

It started with a trickle, a leak so small it was barely noticeable. Still, Gloria Phillips was concerned. She worried that if she didn't do anything, the tiny hole in her roof would grow like a cancer, eventually flooding her house while wreaking havoc on her checkbook.

As luck would have it, Phillips had just seen an advertisement for roof repairs in her local newspaper. Better yet, it promised to fix any leak for just $299. It seemed like a sign from the heavens. She figured it was worth it just for peace of mind.

Phillips called the number and was thrilled when the owner of the company answered the phone himself. Pretty impressive, she thought. If she had any concerns about the company, they were quickly erased when the owner said he was available to come out the very next day to assess the situation. Now that, she thought, was service.

The roofer arrived the next day as promised. He had a look around, scratched his chin, shook his head, mumbled to himself, then proclaimed his "special" roof repair rate wouldn't cover all the work he needed to do. He said the roof was in poor shape and needed new plywood. To do the job right would require a lot of effort—$1,200 worth of effort, to be exact. But don't worry, he said, all of his work is backed by a five-year warranty. If anything happened during that time, anything at all, she'd be covered by the warranty.

Before the man arrived, Phillips was merely concerned about her roof. Now she was downright terrified. Worried her roof was about to cave in, Phillips caved in herself and agreed to the work.

It didn't take her long to realize the error of her ways. Less than a month after the job was completed, Phillips's roof began leaking again. It wasn't just a tiny dribble anymore. Now water was pooling on her floor.

"The roof before, it was just a minor hole," Phillips said. "You could see, like, a wet spot in that area. Once they did the repair, the water started coming in. It was a constant drip. You had to put a bucket there and towels to catch it. They actually made it worse."

Upset, Phillips called the roofing company again and a worker came out to patch the hole with asphalt. That didn't stop the water from seeping through either.

"I called the company again and explained they gave me a five-year warranty in writing on my roof and I needed it fixed," she said. "They hung up the phone on me and have never returned my call."

Subsequent calls went through to an answering machine, which was always full. Then one day a few months later, Phillips called the company's phone number—and found it had been disconnected.

"I'm very angry, very upset," Phillips said. "I've come to

the realization that he never intended to fix my roof. They just scammed me. From the beginning, it was just a scam."

Phillips's story is unfortunately all too common. In the vast sea of contractors, handymen and tradesmen swim with some of the nastiest sharks. While large companies generally fear bad publicity or negative Web posts, small businessmen and contractors often answer to no one but themselves. Many have no corporate rules to abide by, or even a storefront where you can track them down if something goes awry.

Don't get me wrong, there are plenty of fantastic, ethical, highly skilled contractors out there. But odds are that at some point, you'll cross paths with one who cares a whole lot more about taking your money than fixing your house.

Fortunately, there are simple steps you can take to avoid getting scammed by home improvement companies. In many ways, dealing with contractors is no different from dealing with other types of businesses. Being a smart consumer starts with a little bit of research.

Let's take Phillips's story, for example. Why did she think the roofer would be honest? Because it advertised in a trusted place—her local newspaper.

"I said, okay, they're in the paper," she explained. "I'm naïve. I didn't know any better. But I know now it doesn't matter. They all have to be checked out."

A lesson learned the hard way. Had she spent even five minutes on the Internet, Phillips would have seen that the roof repairman was nothing but a shark. The Better Business Bureau logged nine complaints about the business, seven of which the roofer failed to respond to. Among the complaints were service issues, repair issues, warranty issues, and a refund issue.

The BBB gave the company its lowest possible rating, an "F."

Had Phillips logged on to AngiesList.com, an online subscription service in which members rate businesses, she would have found a detailed complaint in which the owner took a $2,600 deposit and did no work.

Angie's List, too, rated the company a big fat "F."

Phillips could have also run a quick search of her local courthouse database to see if anyone had sued the roofing company. In fact, there had been so many complaints about the roofer, that the state had filed a lawsuit charging fraud and deceptive practices.

"I never checked and I should have," Phillips said.

GETTING THE BACKGROUND ON YOUR CONTRACTOR

What resources do consumers have to ensure getting a good contractor? Angie Hicks, founder of the Columbus, Ohio–based Angie's List, recommends taking a step back before hiring any contractor or tradesperson. First talk to friends or family members and ask if they have a recommendation. Back that up with Internet research. If you have a company in mind, search for the company's name and see what others have written about it. Do a quick search on the BBB's website to see if there have been any complaints. If you use a pay service like Angie's List, check it out there, too.

Check to see if the company or tradesman is licensed and

whether he or she has had any run-ins with local regulating agencies. Most states, some counties, and a handful of major cities have websites where you can quickly search licensing information.

New York City, for instance, has a Department of Consumer Affairs where you can file a complaint about a business or ask the department to mediate with the business on your behalf. The department's website also allows you to quickly search to see if a home improvement contractor is licensed with the city. If he or she isn't, there's probably a reason.

In Florida, you can search the state's Department of Business and Professional Regulation. In Texas it's the Department of Licensing and Regulation, and in Idaho, it's the Division of Building Safety. The name of the regulating agency might differ from state to state, but the information is there.

Some states provide more assistance than others. In California, the state's Department of Consumer Affairs offers a license search and a "Complaint Resolution Program," but goes one step further—posting the names and faces of its most notorious unlicensed contractors in a section it calls its "Most Wanted." All of the individuals profiled on the page have warrants issued for their arrests. One recent baddie was wanted for conducting unlicensed tree trimming, which he apparently mixed with rampant methamphetamine use—an odd but potentially wicked combination. Another had fifteen felony charges and six misdemeanors pending against him. Obviously, these are folks you'd rather avoid.

How else can you ensure you won't get taken? If you're embarking on a major project or renovation, get at least three estimates.

"A lot of people really shortchange that aspect of it, but it's really important," Hicks says. "You'd be amazed how wide the estimates can vary."

The cheapest isn't always the best. Ask each contractor for references, then call each of them to hear firsthand about his or her work. It's best to get references from both new jobs and old, so you can inquire about how the work has held up over the years.

Also ask for proof the contractor has insurance. If he or she is hesitant to give you any of the information, that's a pretty serious red flag. It's your money. Do you really want to give it to someone you can't fully trust?

For large projects, some municipalities will require the company to secure a contractor's bond, essentially an insurance policy in case the workers do not complete the job, or do a substandard job. I once received an e-mail from a woman who had paid a contractor $57,000 to install geothermal heating and cooling in her new house. The contractor had screwed things up so royally that the house would not pass inspection.

The woman pleaded with the contractor to come back and make things right. He refused, so she called her city's building department. The man there told her the contractor had been required by the city to take out a $10,000 bond on the work. He helped her file a complaint with the insurance company that administered the bond. After a weeks-long investigation by the insurance company, it gave her the $10,000—enough to hire another contractor to finish the work properly.

If your project isn't large enough to require a bond, it helps if the company you're hiring has a storefront or permanent address. If something goes wrong, it's difficult to complain to a post office box, and as we saw with Phillips, sneaky contractors have a way of ignoring your calls.

When you hire a contractor, never, *ever*, pay the entire cost of the project up front. Once you pay, you've lost your biggest weapon—the threat of withholding money. Most contractors and tradesmen will ask for a deposit, which should be roughly equal to the cost of the supplies. Never pay the deposit in cash. Paying by check or credit card gives you instant proof of payment, and the ability to stop payment should the work hit a sudden snag.

Even after the work starts, hold back some of the payments until everything is complete. At the very end, when it looks like the work is just about done, make a punch list of all the little things that remain. Contractors have a way of moving on to their next project if they've been paid in full and most of the major work is done. By holding back the final payment until you're completely satisfied, you give the contractor some incentive to fully complete the job. Hicks recommends estimating the cost of everything that remains on the punch list, doubling that amount and withholding that much money until everything is done.

Throughout the process, Hicks says, you want to talk regularly with the contractor or tradesman to ensure you're on the same page. Once the work is done, it's much more difficult to change things. If you see something you're not happy with, speak up immediately. It's your house and your money. You have the ultimate say.

I realize this isn't always easy to do. In fact, in some cases, you might not even realize the work is shoddy until, say, your front door falls off its hinges, or your new light fixture begins to spark. And sometimes, especially in emergencies, it's virtually impossible to do the type of research required to find a truly excellent company.

Even the Problem Solver has problems of his own, and while I might be adept at cutting through red tape and corporate doublespeak, I am not what you would call "handy." After my second child was born, I tried for days to install a wooden baby gate at the top of our stairs before throwing in the towel and calling a local fix-it man. It took him roughly five minutes to finish the job, while I stood watching him in embarrassed disbelief. He also hung a large picture frame my wife wouldn't let me touch. She was convinced that if I had put it up myself, it would have eventually crashed to the floor in a spectacular fashion. (It happened once before. Tools, widgets, and doohickeys are not exactly my thing.)

So when water began bubbling up from the drain in my basement floor late one night a few winters ago, I knew I was in trouble. I had just finished running a load of laundry (now *that* I am good at), and as I went to move the clothes from the washer to the dryer, I found myself standing ankle-deep in water.

It was already past 10 p.m., and my regular plumber, whom I've always trusted, had closed up shop hours earlier. But I knew two things for sure: one, ankle-deep water in the basement was a bad thing, and two, I needed immediate help. Besides that, it smelled. So I logged on to the Internet, ignored all common sense and good judgment, and called the first twenty-four-hour plumber I could find.

Two hours later, a man I had never met pulled up in a van, came into my house, and surveyed the situation. Just like the roofer Phillips had hired, the plumber shook his head. He tsk-tsked. He mumbled some incoherent plumberspeak. To be honest, he had me a bit freaked out.

He told me I had a serious plumbing problem. Who was I to argue? My feet were soaking wet. He said there was nothing he could do that night, but that he would come back in the morning and clean out the catch basin. He handed me an estimate that said it would take him and a partner more than two hours to complete the work, at a cost of $450. Standing in that puddle of mucky water, I probably would have agreed to roughly five times that amount, plus a home-cooked meal and a massage. I just wanted my pipes fixed.

The next day, he came back and started up some machine that made an ungodly sound. I was gone for work when he finished—only forty-five minutes after he'd started. Despite working less than half the time he said the job would take, he still insisted on the $450. My wife promptly cut him a check.

By the time I came home from work, I had come to my senses. I called my regular plumber, who came by the next day to take a look. He quickly determined that the fly-by-night plumber had done virtually nothing to clean out the catch basin. My regular plumber then proceeded to finish the job—for a mere $190.

What should I have done? Well, first of all, I should have remained calm, even as the water was rising. Had I taken my own advice and checked the Internet, I would have immediately found two complaints lodged against the plumber with the BBB, which gave him a "C" rating. Not exactly a ringing endorsement. In fact, I would not have found any kind words about the man anywhere on the World Wide Web. It cost me $450, but I learned an important lesson: don't panic.

Hicks recommends doing a little homework ahead of time—reconnaissance, as it were—for tradesmen you might need in an emergency: plumbers, electricians, heating and cooling experts, carpenters, and others. Keep a list of companies you've vetted and can trust, including businesses that are open twenty-four hours a day, so that when something goes wrong, you don't find yourself dialing businesses blindly, as I had done that night.

"Things like that happen," Hicks said. "Having someone in mind ahead of time really helps."

Now, before you lose all faith in my problem-solving, no-holds-barred, get-tough philosophy, let me add a quick side note to my horrific plumbing experience. After my regular plumber left, I immediately called the fly-by-night plumber and read him the riot act. I must say, I was nervous. I'm not a huge fan of confrontation.

I laid out the facts, saying a plumber I trust reviewed his work and declared it shoddy. I told him I knew he did almost no work. He protested at first, but I had some talking points that I had gleaned from my regular plumber. I told him I had seen the catch basin before my plumber started his work, and then again after. I threatened to file complaints with my village, the state attorney general, the Better Business Bureau, and the local media. He quickly caved. He said he wanted to keep his good name and "make things right." He asked how much money I wanted back. I realized he had done some work—he showed up at my house in the middle of the night, after all—so I told him to keep what he truly earned and send me a check for the remainder.

Less than a week later, a $200 check arrived in the mail.

REMEMBER:

* Ask neighbors and friends for recommendations on plumbers, electricians, and other home improvement contractors.
* Follow up all recommendations with research of your own. Check the Better Business Bureau, Angie's List, state and local regulating agencies, and even your local courthouse.
* Make sure the contractor is licensed.
* Ask for a contract in writing.
* Never pay for the work in cash, and never pay the entire amount up front.
* Stay in constant contact with the contractor while the

work is being done. It's better than being surprised at the end.

* Withhold some money until the entire project is done. Make sure everything is completed exactly how you desire.
* For major projects, see if the company is required to take out a construction bond.
* Do your research ahead of time and keep a list of contractors you can call in an emergency.
* If you do have an emergency, don't panic. Even five minutes of research can help you avoid larger problems down the road.

7

THE PEOPLE'S COURT
Navigating Small Claims Court

At this point in the book, it might seem like I'm using the airlines as poster children for crappy customer service. For that, I apologize . . . but I'm not done quite yet. You see, I'd be remiss if I neglected to tell you the story of one John Villafranco, a Washington, D.C., attorney who boarded a plane several years ago wanting nothing more than an uneventful holiday out west.

He made it home safely. His luggage did not.

After several days, a courier arrived at the doorstep of his Georgetown home carrying a hefty bag. Inside were the remains of his poor suitcase. Villafranco opened the bag to discover his clothing had been literally beaten to death. As a bonus, there was mangled clothing he did not recognize—shirts and pants from some other star-crossed soul who had the unhappy circumstance of passing through the Denver airport that same week.

Sound familiar? Bear with me. This story is a wee bit different.

After collecting what remained of his (and someone else's) belongings, Villafranco called the airline, which offered him a few measly travel vouchers that in no way equaled the total amount of his loss, about $1,000.

Villafranco politely told the customer service agent no, and asked again to be fully reimbursed for his lost and damaged clothing.

"They said I had to have receipts for each article of clothing," Villafranco recalled. "I asked the guy, 'What are you wearing right now? Do you have receipts for it?'"

He might have earned style points for his clever retort, but Villafranco's approach did little to convince the airline to cut him a check.

"Not having any receipts, I was out of luck," he said.

Well, almost. As I mentioned before, Villafranco is a lawyer, and not just any kind of lawyer. He specializes in consumer protection. So he did what any good lawyer would do.

He sued the airline in small claims court.

I've already discussed myriad strategies for cutting through bureaucracy and corporate red tape. I've talked about agencies that are available to help if you run into a brick wall, and effective ways for arguing your case. I've outlined methods for scaring a business into correcting a mistake, and highlighted the importance of voting with your checkbook. But the cold hard truth is that sometimes, none of that works, which leaves you with two simple options.

1. You can give up.
2. You can sue.

As you've probably gathered by now, I'm not a huge fan of Option One.

To be clear, I'm not saying we should get all sue-happy.

Lord knows our courts are already clogged with frivolous law-suits. Litigation should always be the remedy of last resort, the option you invoke when pleading, screaming, cajoling, and all other manner of badgering fails. But if a company has screwed you over and absolutely won't listen to reason, you might be left with no other recourse. You'd be surprised how effective a little court action can be.

For the uninitiated (those of you who, like me, are not an attorney and have never been on either side of a lawsuit), the small claims process can appear intimidating. It truly isn't. By its very definition, small claims branches are the people's court—without a cantankerous Judge Wapner or Judge Judy.

Remember in earlier chapters when I told you that to win against corporations and businesses, you have to first convince them that not helping you will cost them more in the long run? Well, filing a lawsuit pretty much grabs a company by its lapels and screams, "Get out your checkbook, sucker!"

The mere act of filing a claim is often enough. In Villa-franco's case, he filed his lawsuit in the District of Columbia's small claims court. He was pretty sure he would win, given that the airline ripped his luggage to shreds. Still, even when they are at fault, many airlines don't like to provide reimbursement unless absolutely forced to. Villafranco's lawsuit provided just that force.

On the night before the lawsuit was scheduled for a hear-ing, an attorney for the airline called Villafranco and said the company wanted to settle.

"I explained to him I felt the law was pretty solidly on my side here," Villafranco said. "I said I'd go to court the next day."

Smart move. Villafranco knew lawsuits were expensive. He knew that even in small claims court, a company would have to send an attorney as representation. If no one showed up for the company, the judge could enter a default judgment in Villafranco's favor, forcing the company to pay up, perhaps more than it would have paid in a settlement. And sending an attorney, it turns out, isn't cheap. The company's lawyer would probably have had to sit around the courthouse for a few hours waiting for the case to be called, happily collecting some ungodly hourly fee while twiddling his or her thumbs.

When Villafranco refused to back down, the airline's attorney asked him what he wanted. He asked for full compensation for his roughly $1,000 worth of shredded clothing along with payment of the fees associated with the small claims filing.

The airline caved.

"The lesson really is—and I represent mostly corporations, not consumers—small claims can be a very effective tool for consumers because the corporation will have to defend itself, and it's very costly," Villafranco said. "Frequently, from what I find in my own experience, if you have a gripe as a consumer against a company, just by virtue of filing a complaint, you have gotten their attention. . . . Your leverage is that court date."

TAKING IT TO COURT

So how does it work? In most small claims cases you represent yourself, since hiring an attorney would cost you more than you'd probably recoup. The rules vary in different cities, counties, and states, but there is always a cap on the amount you can sue for. In some small claims courts, the cap is a mere $1,500. In some parts of Tennessee, you can sue for up to $25,000.

If your dispute involves a significant amount of money, you should check your court's rules to ensure your lawsuit does not exceed the threshold. In fact, most small claims courts provide a booklet outlining its rules and procedures, using comprehensible language intended for nonlawyers.

In most cases, the courts provide a form on which you can write your complaint. Keep your complaint short, factual, and backed up by as much documentation as you can muster. Copy the documents and attach them to the complaint as exhibits for your case.

Filing a lawsuit isn't free. The fees vary from court to court, but in most cases it will cost you anywhere from $50 to $200 to file. As I mentioned before, with any luck, merely filing the lawsuit will be enough to convince the company to pay you, but always assume your claim will go to a hearing and prepare accordingly. If you win, ask the judge to make the defendant pay your filing fees.

If a company or business offers you a settlement to avoid a court hearing, get it in writing. A verbal commitment is worthless. The last thing you want to do is drop your lawsuit, then have the business back out on its promise, leaving you with nothing—and out the cost of the filing fee.

When filing a lawsuit, you must serve the person you are suing. Essentially, that means you must deliver paperwork about the suit to the person or the business. The rules vary by state and county, but in some jurisdictions, you can pay the local sheriff's department to serve the papers. In other places, you can pay a process server to do the dirty work.

Some small claims courts allow you to serve the papers yourself, either by certified mail or in person. To get an address for the owner, president, or representative of the business you are suing, check with your state to find the company's articles of incorporation, which generally contain either the owner or a registered agent.

If a company is publicly traded, try searching its profit-reporting statement, which is filed with the federal Security and Exchange Commission. You can also find the information on the company's investor-relations webpage, or sometimes through a simple Google search. Of course, if you send the papers by certified mail and the recipient refuses to accept it, you're back at square one and you will probably have to pay for the services of a process server or your local sheriff. If you're confused about the process or have questions about what documents are required, ask your local court.

If your case gets before a judge, you'll be asked to summarize your complaint. In most instances you won't have much time, so start with the most important information first. In journalism, we call this "inverted pyramid style," meaning you pack your first few sentences with the who, what, why, when, and where, then fill in the details farther down. Generally, you'll be given only a few minutes to speak. Use your time wisely.

Be concise, get to the point quickly, and say exactly what you want. Don't get greedy, ask only for what you are owed, and keep your emotions in check. While getting all lathered up on the phone might get you somewhere with a customer service agent, it will get you nowhere with a judge. Stay calm, be truthful, and back up your claims with as much evidence as you can find. Make three copies of every document you plan to present in court: one for the judge, one for the opposition, and one for yourself.

Most of all, don't freak out. This isn't the Supreme Court and nobody expects you to reference detailed case law. Don't pretend to be something you're not. While you should do a little research to make sure the law is on your side, you don't need to cite code and verse of federal, state, or local law.

"Don't go in there and try to be Perry Mason and pretend to be a lawyer and speak like a lawyer," Villafranco said. "Speak plainly. If there's a mistake that's made, it's when a consumer thinks they need to take a crash law school course and speak like a lawyer."

Derek Monroe is no lawyer. In fact, he has no legal training at all. Yet the father of two is the self-proclaimed King of Small Claims Court. Over the past several years, Monroe has filed more than fifty small claims lawsuits against some of the biggest companies in America.

When Pizza Hut wouldn't honor his son's Reading Award Certificate for a free personal pan pizza, he sued. When his new eyeglasses from America's Best Contacts & Eyeglasses fell apart a few days after he bought them, he sued again. When Air France damaged his luggage and did not sufficiently make amends . . . well, you get the picture.

He's won or reached a favorable settlement in more than

half of his cases, often getting the companies to not only pay him, but to write formal apologies. On rare occasion, he's even gotten a company to change its business practices. He views small claims court as a great leveler, a way for all the Davids of the world to aim their legal slingshots at the hulking Goliaths.

"The only thing that brings me hope is the justice system in this country still works for the little guy," Monroe said. "No matter who you are or how little money you have, the legal system can help you."

In one case, Monroe went to his local grocery store and, among other things, purchased a $34.23 box of teeth-whitening strips. It wasn't until he arrived home that he read the fine print on the box. Turns out, the whitening strips had expired . . . four years earlier. Yuck.

Monroe still had his receipt and he hadn't opened the box, so he drove right back to the store and asked for a refund. When a store employee refused, Monroe gathered up his paperwork and filed a lawsuit.

Let me say right here, I don't necessarily advocate filing a small claims suit over $34.23—especially if you haven't al- ready exhausted other avenues for getting your money back. Of course, for Monroe it wasn't about the money, it was the prin- ciple of the thing. The grocery store *should* have refunded his money immediately. But filing a lawsuit, even in small claims court, has its costs. In Monroe's case, his filing fees alone cost more than he stood to gain, and that doesn't figure in the cost of his time. Even assuming his hourly rate at minimum wage, Monroe stood to lose significantly if the judge ruled against him.

In this case, that wasn't really the point. Monroe insists it is important to keep companies honest, not just for yourself but for other consumers as well. True enough.

In his lawsuit against the grocery store, officially titled Monroe v. SuperValue, Inc., the company fought the case in court. It took three and a half months to wend its way through the system, but Monroe won. A panel of arbitrators ordered SuperValue, Inc., to give Monroe his money—plus his costs for filing suit.

One of his secret weapons, he said, is to use a company's own words or policies against it.

"Whenever possible, I go to the company's website and print out the company's code of ethics," he said. "I present it in court. I don't want to sound cynical or bitter, but the longer the ethics code is, the worse the company generally is when it comes to customer service."

Perhaps the most important rule, Monroe said, is to stick to your guns. Never be intimidated.

"Just be forthright and honest," he said.

If you're right, the judge will see that.

"Don't fear the process," Villafranco said. "It's a process that is intended to be friendly to your average consumer. It's not a process that's intended for lawyers. If you have a gripe and you're unable to get satisfaction through conversations with customer service agents, it's worth a try."

REMEMBER:

* Ask your small claims court if it has a pamphlet outlining the rules and procedures of the court. Study it well before filing a complaint.
* Make sure your claim does not exceed the court's limits, which range from $1,500 to $25,000, depending on where you live.
* Ask about filing fees, which range from $50 to about $200.
* Write your complaint accurately and concisely. Proofread it carefully for accuracy, typos, and name spellings.
* Research the law, but don't try to be Perry Mason. The system is set up for laypeople. You don't have to know the law inside and out.
* Find a name and address for the CEO or registered agent for the company so you can serve him or her with the lawsuit.
* If a company offers to settle, get it in writing.
* While in court, stay calm. This is a low-key affair.
* Be concise. You won't have much time to make your argument.
* If the company has a code of conduct, print it out and present it in court.
* Most important of all, be honest. Judges have notoriously strong BS detectors.

8

POWER STRUGGLE
Battling the Big, Bad Utilities

Vito Grimaldi feared his electric bills. Every month he opened the envelope and braced for the worst. Based on the eye-popping numbers, Grimaldi sensed something was amiss, but he couldn't be sure. He ran a Ben & Jerry's ice cream shop, after all: he knew it took a lot of power to keep his tubs of Chunky Monkey and Cherry Garcia frozen.

He had long assumed the two meters listed on his monthly bill were for two different parts of his store—the freezers and the dining area. But as his bills continued to mount, so did his doubts. When an electrician came to fix some wiring, Grimaldi asked the man to check out the meters. The electrician opened the door to the mall's utility room and immediately identified the problem. One of the meters on Grimaldi's bill was for his store, but the other serviced a restaurant next door.

Grimaldi called his power company, Commonwealth Edison, and asked for an investigation. The utility took its time sending out a technician. When one finally arrived more than a month later, he confirmed the electrician's assessment. The second meter was indeed for another store.

A few days later, ComEd called Grimaldi with a less-than-generous offer. The electric company said it would credit his account for two months' worth of electricity. Grimaldi smartly said no. He had been inappropriately charged for the neighboring restaurant's electric use since the day he opened his ice cream store more than four years earlier. He said he wanted to be reimbursed for everything—all four years of overpayments. Running the numbers quickly in his head, Grimaldi surmised that the electric company owed him thousands of dollars.

Months passed and he heard nothing from ComEd. Convinced he was being stonewalled, Grimaldi brushed up on his state's utility laws, reading the statutes top to bottom. He discovered that ComEd was legally bound to give back every penny he had overpaid. To his credit, he had kept original copies of all his utility bills, dating all the way back to the day his store opened.

He made copies of everything. He printed out the pertinent statutes and highlighted his bills. He called ComEd repeatedly. Repeatedly, ComEd stonewalled.

So Grimaldi figured out which state agency regulated utility companies—in his case the state's commerce commission—and filed a complaint against ComEd.

That got ComEd's attention. Days later, the electric company responded again, this time offering a credit for five months worth of service. Again, Grimaldi said no. He told ComEd he knew his rights and he wouldn't settle for anything less than a full refund.

When no one called him back, he phoned the utility's customer service center. A customer service agent told him he had to call the corporate offices. The corporate offices patched him back through to customer service. And so it went.

By then, he had reached his boiling point. Mount Grimaldi was ready to explode.

"I called the customer service line and talked to a woman there," he said. "I kind of got irate with her. I said, 'This has been going on since August and now it's January.' I can be an SOB when I have to be. A lot of people won't do that."

He proceeded to tell the customer service agent that he was a small business owner and that paying his neighbor's electric bill simply wasn't fair. He fumed. He fussed. After a while, the customer service agent put Grimaldi on hold. When she got back on, she spoke in hushed tones.

"She said, 'I'm going to give you some information I shouldn't be giving you. Don't say it came from me,'" Grimaldi later recalled. "She gave me the name and number for the person at ComEd who handles commerce commission complaints."

Bingo. Grimaldi had obtained a golden ticket—a direct dial phone number for a muckety-muck deep inside the power company, a man normally protected by seemingly impenetrable layers of by-the-book customer service agents, a man who had the ability to make actual decisions.

Grimaldi thanked the woman, hung up, and called the number she had given him.

"The first thing he said was, 'How did you get my number?'" Grimaldi said.

In one fell swoop, Grimaldi had applied all of the concepts we've talked about—research, getting nasty when necessary, never giving up, and more. He had to. He wasn't just dealing with any old company, he was dealing with a utility, a company that had a monopoly on his business—and acted like it.

MONOPOLY MONEY

Unlike other businesses, utilities are immune to the consumer's ultimate weapon: the threat of leaving. You can't just tell the electric company, "Correct my bill or I'm taking my business elsewhere." In this case, "elsewhere" is a place lit only by candlelight. Grimaldi had no alternative source of power. His options were ComEd or a store filled with room-temperature Triple Caramel Chunk.

That's why states have established certain protections to ensure you have a fighting chance against monopolistic utility companies. All states have utility commissions that help regulate the industry and, in some cases, handle individual complaints. Many states also have nonprofit agencies designed specifically to keep watch over gas, electric, water, and telecommunications companies. Almost all of the watchdog agencies will advocate on your behalf if you have a problem with a utility.

With utilities, the first difficulty to overcome is knowing whether there's a problem. In Grimaldi's case, he sensed something was wrong, but it was not immediately obvious. After all, it was plausible his store had two meters. In fact, the only sure way to get a feel for what your bill should be is to always, always read it religiously.

This especially holds true if you've gone green and have quit receiving paper bills. That's noble of you, and I wholeheartedly support your efforts to save the environment. But what's great news for the planet's future is not necessarily good for your bank account. A byproduct of switching to e-bills and automatic payment plans is that many people have simply quit reading their monthly statements. Without reading your statements, you have no idea if something has gone terribly wrong—or even not-so-terribly wrong.

If you live in a multiunit building (or in Grimaldi's case, own a store in a multibusiness building), check to make sure your meter matches up to the meter number on your bill. You'd be amazed how often meters are accidentally switched. The last thing you want to do is pay for your neighbor cranking his or her air conditioner all summer while you're sweating it out with the thermostat at seventy-eight degrees, perplexed about how your electric bill remains so high.

If you don't check your bill, you'll never know if a utility company has tacked on an unwanted and usually unnecessary service, like a "protection plan" or "line-backing service." The charges might seem small on a monthly basis, but they add up over time.

"It's amazing how much information is in the bill if you actually take a look at it," said Mindy Spatt, spokeswoman for the Utility Reform Network, a nonprofit watchdog group based in San Francisco. "You should look at it every month."

When you're done reading your bills, save them. That way if a bill suddenly seems out of whack, you have a baseline of past bills to compare it to. If your July bill this year is twice what it was last year, you have a pretty good idea that something is wrong. Never trust that the utility company will keep your records for you. The law varies in different states, but there is generally a limit to how long a utility must keep your monthly bills on file. In some states, utilities can destroy records that exceed two years old. Even if they are required to keep your records longer, it's always easier to have your own copies if there is a dispute. Getting a utility to pony up copies of your past statements can be both frustrating and time consuming.

If you think something is wrong with your bill, speak up. Spatt says far too many people simply ignore their problems, either cowed by the big, bad utility company or out of sheer laziness. Don't be lazy. And by all means, don't be scared. If you don't stick up for yourself, who will?

"Document, then complain," Spatt said. "I think a lot of times people just suck it up when they need to speak out."

Religiously reading your bill is a good first step. So is learning how to read your meters. In most cases, utility companies will post on their websites instructions on how to read the meter's numbers. If you live in an apartment building and don't have access to your meter, ask the building manager or maintenance worker to let you in. Or schedule an appointment with your utility company to have one of its employees show you your meter. Make sure the numbers on your meter jibe with the numbers on your bill. Mistakes happen. Meter readers are, after all, human.

Learning to read your own meter is especially important if your utility company uses "estimated" billing, a practice designed to save the company money by cutting the frequency by which an employee is actually dispatched to your house for a reading. Instead of an actual reading, the company simply estimates how much it thinks you have used.

Estimated readings can be a recipe for disaster. If your usage is overestimated, you wind up paying more than you actually owe. If it's underestimated, you often wind up making up for that down the road with a so-called balloon payment—a huge bill that makes up for the previous low estimates. Either way, you're better off paying exactly what you owe, nothing more, nothing less. Many utilities will allow you to call in your meter readings yourself, protecting you from potentially inaccurate bills.

If you do encounter a problem, try calling your utility company first. In most cases, the utility will investigate on its own and resolve the issue.

If that doesn't work, file a complaint with your state's utility regulator, like Grimaldi did. Every state has a regulating agency. The rules vary depending on where you live, and some regulators (often called utility commissions) are more consumer friendly than others. But all of them have a direct line to the utility companies, and most will provide assistance if you ask for it. (For a full list, visit the National Association of State Utility Advocates website at NASUCA.org.)

"Most cases are resolved with a phone call to the commission and the commission bucking it back to the utility company," said Gerald Norlander, executive director of the Public Utility Law Project in New York. "Usually the utility has the burden to respond and explain to the regulator that what they did was reasonable and within their rules."

If you don't know the rules governing utilities in your state—and really, who does?—ask. While many utility companies are required to inform customers of their rights every year, they usually do so by attaching a pamphlet or form to one of your bills. You can identify this mailing by one of two telltale signs: (1) it's in microprint so small that it takes a magnifying glass held over a microscope to read it, or (2) even if you devise some way to actually read the tiny little letters, the words make absolutely no sense.

Your best bet is checking with your state utility commission or a nonprofit watchdog group in your area. They know the nuances of utility law in your state, and can usually explain it in a way that consumers can understand.

Sometimes, detecting problems can take a little sleuthing. If you think your electric bill is too high, locate your meter and turn on and off lights or appliances. If it doesn't seem that your usage correlates with the meter reading, you might have a legitimate complaint.

"Mistakes happen," Norlander said. "These are big systems, the computer systems, the billing systems. There are large numbers of pieces of equipment. A lot of it sits outside in pretty nasty weather. I mean, how well would your computer do nailed to a wall outside during a winter in Chicago?"

For those of you not from Chicago, I can assure you: not well.

Of course, not all mistakes are equipment issues. I once got a call from the nurse of a disabled man named Terry Koehler, who had had his electricity turned off for nonpayment. Koehler had recently received a $942 grant that was supposed to ensure his power kept flowing, but the electric company failed to apply the grant to his account.

None of Koehler's calls to the electric company seemed to help. Each time he was told there was no record of the $942 payment and without it, his power would remain off. I advised him to file a complaint with the Citizens Utility Board, a nonprofit agency established to protect consumers' rights. Six hours after Koehler filed his complaint with the Citizens Utility Board, the electric company called to say it had located his missing money. Two hours after that, his power was turned back on.

"Suddenly after CUB called them, oh gee, lo and behold, they were able to find the $942 they had for two weeks and they were able to get it posted to my account," Koehler told me. "The Citizens Utility Board called it in as an emergency complaint. That got them moving."

David Kolata, CUB's executive director, said it's imperative to use all available resources when fighting a utility. Don't bravely try to go it alone, especially when help is available. Utility commissions and watchdog groups are better at navigating the system than individual consumers.

"Having someone to advocate for you and share your experience, that's important," Kolata said. "They have direct lines to utilities and can usually find people there who, if they don't always solve your problem, you at least don't have to play phone tree."

Kolata said his organization handles thousands of complaints a year about utility companies, which he believes represents just the tip of the iceberg.

"I think big companies often assume that it's such a big hassle that you won't go through with it," he said.

Not Vito Grimaldi. When we last checked in with him, the ice cream shop owner had just spoken to someone at the electric company whose desk sat in the mythical office land located deep behind the Great Wall of Customer Service. After their conversation, ComEd sent another technician out to verify yet again that the second meter was not Grimaldi's (utilities, like most big businesses, do not part with their money easily).

The good news is, Grimaldi's efforts paid off. After all his well-researched griping, he was issued a refund for the entire time he was overbilled, all the way back to the day he opened his shop. Because he had copies of all his utility bills, the electric company had no leg to stand on. The grand total of his refund was more than $5,000.

What did Grimaldi learn from the experience?

"I never had a high opinion of any of the utility companies to begin with," he said. "The way they've dealt with me, I'd never trust them again on anything. You have to double check everything.

"I'm a little more tenacious than some people might be," he continued. "Most people, if they were told they would get a five-month refund, would just give up on it after a while. I just wasn't going to give up on it."

That's a healthy attitude.

"It's going to save me a lot of money," he told me. The last time I checked with him, he hadn't paid an electric bill in nine months.

REMEMBER:

* Research utility laws in your state. The more you know about your rights, the less likely you are to get taken advantage of.
* Once you know your rights, defend them.
* Check your bills thoroughly. If anything seems out of whack, call the utility company immediately.
* Learn how to read your own meters, and if you live in a multiunit building, make sure the meter you're paying for actually services your apartment.
* Keep copies of your statements in case there is a dispute.
* If a utility company won't listen to you, file a complaint with your state's utility commission, or with a nonprofit watchdog group.
* Be tenacious. Utilities might hold a monopoly, but that doesn't mean they have to be bullies.

9

UNCIVIL SERVANTS
Getting Your Government to Work for You

When she walked into hearing room 103, Sandra Sahi was understandably apprehensive. She had never been in a courtroom before.

A few months earlier, Sahi had received a $100 ticket in the mail for running a red light. A camera mounted at the intersection allegedly caught her in the act. The ticket came with time-stamped pictures of her car running the light, but to Sahi, the pictures told a different story. For one thing, it was clear the light was yellow, not red, when she entered the intersection. Then there was the fact that Sahi was turning right, and there were no signs prohibiting such a move.

She requested a hearing to contest the ticket. That led her to a stark, windowless hearing room on Chicago's Near West Side one hot summer morning. Presiding over the tiny courtroom was administrative law judge Taryn Springs, a stern but fair woman with an encyclopedic knowledge of municipal traffic code.

It didn't take Springs long to realize the ticket was issued in error. After reviewing the pictures, the computer-generated citation, and Sahi's evidence, Springs ruled the city failed to meet its burden of proof. It took less than two minutes for Springs to proclaim, "Case dismissed."

Sahi left the courtroom wearing a wide smile.

"I'm feeling great," she said. "The system worked."

Amazingly, shockingly, astonishingly, it really does. Sometimes, anyway. We've all heard the old saying "you can't fight city hall," but the truth of the matter is, you can. You just have to be smart about it.

Let's start with the simple parking ticket.

Few things in life are as frustrating—or as universal. I'm guessing you've probably returned from a haircut or a shopping trip to find a ticket shoved under your windshield wiper or affixed with industrial-strength goo to your driver's-side window. If you live in a major metropolis, parking tickets are almost unavoidable. The city of New York alone issues millions of tickets a year, and they aren't cheap.

The fine for parking at an expired meter in Manhattan is $65. Park in a bus lane and it will cost you $115. The city can nab you on any of eighty infractions written into its parking code, and if there isn't an infraction that specifically fits your case, an officer can write you up for violating Code 99, which the city defines as "all other parking, standing, or stopping violations."

Sheesh.

"It's pretty huge," said Haskell Nussbaum, a former New York parking ticket judge. "It's a heck of a moneymaker for the city."

Nussbaum was so enthralled by the enormity of the system, he wrote a book about it: *Beat That Parking Ticket.*

His first piece of advice? Contest every ticket—even the ones you think you have no chance of overturning. Why? Nussbaum says that up to a quarter of all handwritten parking tickets he ruled on and perhaps 10 percent of electronic tickets are entered incorrectly, meaning the wrong box was marked, numbers were accidentally transposed, or some key bit of information was inadvertently omitted. Those errors create small technical defects that can convince a judge to throw your ticket out.

In some cases, you might not even realize the ticket was written incorrectly, but an administrative law judge can spot the error immediately.

"Most people, I think, just pay up," Nussbaum said. "If you don't play, you don't win."

In most cities, you are given the option of challenging a ticket online, through the mail, or in person. If you have the time, always appear in person. That allows you to answer a hearing officer's questions, something you can't do by mail. You can also clarify your argument and provide credibility to your case.

I once wrote about a man named Mark Geinosky, who, for reasons he still doesn't know, was written two dozen bogus parking tickets by Chicago police officers over the course of sixteen months. He was cited repeatedly for infractions like parking in a crosswalk, parking too close to a fire hydrant, or obstructing the roadway.

Geinosky swore he didn't commit any of the violations. In fact, he said neither he nor his car were present at any of the cited locations. Each time he received a batch of tickets in the mail (sometimes, the notices arrived four at a time), Geinosky trudged down to the courthouse with a file folder filled with evidence.

His hard work paid off. He was able to get all twenty-four of the tickets thrown out. Every single one of them.

"I think it's better to go in person because the judge gets to see how serious you are," Geinosky said.

Needless to say, he's logged a little quality time in traffic court. He, too, could probably write a book.

"I've listened to all the people who have gone in there hoping to get a ticket dismissed," Geinosky said. "What I noticed is if you're there and you're polite, they tried to work with you."

What else did he learn? Dress up. You don't have to wear a suit and tie (although Geinosky often did), but make sure your jeans aren't ripped and your T-shirt doesn't say anything offensive.

"Be respectful," Geinosky said. "A lot of people go to court wearing what they're wearing to the beach. It really doesn't make sense to me. It tells the hearing officer you're not really all that serious about this."

If you have a choice, go early in the week or midweek. That way, if the hearing officer asks for documentation you don't have, you can ask for the case to be continued while you run home and get it. Some judges will let you leave and come back later, either that day or later in the week. Other judges forbid it. But it's always worth trying.

Never interrupt the judge and never raise your voice. In courtroom 103, Judge Springs did not take too kindly to defendants' arguments that the parking ticket system sucked, or that the process was "[expletive] crazy."

In fact, it's a pretty good idea to just leave the expletives at home.

"People get all upset and say all kinds of things," Nussbaum said. "People don't remember that the judges don't have power to set policy. They're only really there to adjudicate the ticket. But people are people and that includes the judges."

So it's best not to offend them. In fact, in some cities, judges have the authority to give you a break if they feel that even though you've violated the law, there were extenuating circumstances. So if you received a $100 ticket for parking in a loading zone, but you did so because your wife was nine months pregnant and going into labor, the judge might find you guilty but reduce the fine to, say, $25.

The bottom line? Getting irate can help you cut through the static on a customer service call, but it rarely convinces a judge to help you. So be nice.

If you cannot attend a hearing in person, by all means contest the ticket by mail, and be as thorough as possible. If you're asked to write your argument on the ticket sleeve and there's not enough space, continue writing on a separate piece of paper and attach it. Try to anticipate questions a judge might have and provide the appropriate answers.

Attach all pertinent evidence, and don't be afraid to go a bit overboard. It's better to include too much information than to have the hearing officer rule against you due to lack of evidence. If you're taking pictures of a street sign, take pictures of the entire block. Put the scene in context. Show the judge a complete view of why the ticket was incorrectly issued, and explain in writing exactly what you think the pictures show.

"Half the time, it's the photos that will tell the story better than you will," Nussbaum said.

KNOW THY ELECTED OFFICIALS

Of course, governmental agencies don't just issue parking tickets. They also tax us, fix our roads, remove our garbage, provide health insurance when we grow old, and do a gazillion other things that improve our lives—and aggravate us—on a daily basis.

Government is great when it functions smoothly. But when things go wrong, watch out. Breaking through the many layers of bureaucracy and red tape can seem like an exercise in futility. Standing in line at the DMV can feel like a 1980s Soviet bread line. Getting a new driver's license shouldn't take hours. And have you ever tried calling the IRS? You might as well be calling Hal 9000. There are so many keypad prompts, the tip of your dialing finger just about goes numb. On one recent call, I spent several minutes typing before the automated voice told me to hang up and dial a different number. Gee, thanks.

It doesn't have to be so frustrating.

As a general rule, when dealing with governmental agencies, seek out the appropriate elected official. A faceless customer service agent or middle manager in your city's waste-management department might not care if your trash is picked up on time, but your city council representative will. The reason is simple. The bureaucrat doesn't need your vote in the next election, but the councilman does. It's never a bad idea to remind elected officials who keeps them in office.

Unfortunately, your vote alone isn't always enough to convince an elected official to help you. Often, to get his or her attention, you have to multiply the threat. I once received an e-mail from a man named Worlee Glover, who had endured an unsightly and unsafe hole in the parkway in front of his house for weeks. It seemed the city's water department had fixed a pipe under the road, but did nothing to clean up the mess when it was done. The work crew simply packed up its equipment and left.

A mound of dirt sat untouched in Glover's yard, collecting candy wrappers and twenty-ounce soda bottles from the kids who passed each day on their way to and from a nearby school. What really upset Glover was the city's haphazard attempt to mitigate the danger. At some point, crews had placed a few sheets of flimsy plywood over the hole. Glover called the city repeatedly to get the hole filled and the dirt mound removed. He worried a child would get hurt.

Upset that the city wasn't responding, Glover upped the ante. He took out his camera and snapped pictures of the unsightly mess. He found a Facebook page devoted to issues in his neighborhood and started posting the pictures every day. With each picture, Glover included the number of days the hole had been left untouched, along with a message for his councilwoman, who frequently posted information on that page. He asked in plain, simple language why she hadn't done anything to get the hole fixed.

The pictures touched a nerve. Some of Glover's neighbors

began posting their own comments about the situation. After a few days, the councilwoman contacted Glover directly. The hole was soon filled.

The Internet has made it easier than ever to give voice to your complaint. Few people are as thin-skinned or self-conscious as politicians. Whenever possible, use their neuroses to your benefit. Nothing motivates an elected official more than the thought of losing his or her next election. And that concept holds true at every level—municipal, county, state, and federal.

Of course, the layers of bureaucracy grow thicker at each stop along the way. Let's take the Social Security Administration as an example. At some point we'll all have to deal with this mega agency. The good news is, because of its sheer size, it offers multiple points of entry. With baby boomers fast approaching retirement age, the number of people receiving Social Security benefits is growing by millions every year. The agency has vastly improved its website to handle the crush of new recipients, making it possible to apply for most benefits online.

Experts say that, for the most part, dealing with Social Security via the Internet is safe, painless, and effective. But, as was the case with parking tickets, it's always better to deal with the issue in person if you run into a problem or want to dispute something.

If you plan to visit your local Social Security office and want to avoid long lines, go midweek and midmonth, when there are likely to be fewer people dealing with check-related issues. Most people visit federal offices before work or during lunch, so, if possible, visit in late morning or early afternoon. And call ahead and schedule an appointment if you can. The same principles hold true for many government agencies.

If you apply for disability through Social Security and are denied, do not get discouraged. Experts say most applications are initially turned down, but if you are truly disabled and you continue appealing the decision, you likely will win in the end. I must warn you, it's usually not a particularly fun or easy process. Most people are not only denied on their initial application, but again when they request a reconsideration of the denial.

Keep fighting. Your case will be heard before an administrative law judge if you continue to pursue it. At that level, many people are finally approved.

"Overall, people are intimidated by the Social Security Administration because they don't get good answers on the phone or it's hard to find good information," said John Tucker, a Clearwater, Florida–based attorney who handles disability cases. "Unfortunately, you're just going to have to deal with the system."

Tucker says it's vitally important to appeal a Social Security denial within the prescribed sixty days. If you're nearing the deadline, walk your paperwork to the nearest Social Security office and hand it over in person.

In previous chapters we've discussed the importance of keeping detailed records of phone calls and copies of all correspondence. That's especially true when dealing with huge bureaucracies like Social Security, where one employee you talk to might have no idea what another employee has said.

If all else fails, fall back on seeking help from an elected official, in this case your congressperson. Every congressional office has a team devoted to helping constituents deal with issues such as these, and that team will have a direct contact within the Social Security Administration—or any other federal agency.

"That can be very helpful," Tucker said. "Usually, they'll send an inquiry."

If your gripe concerns a state agency, contact your state senator or representative. If you've got a problem with city government, visit your councilman's office. As is always the case, it's better to visit the office in person, if possible. It never hurts to remind your elected officials why they're there—to represent you and your concerns.

Sometimes, that's all it takes. As a voter, you possess a lot of power. Use it.

REMEMBER:

* Contest every parking ticket, even the ones you think you probably won't win. Even a small mistake by the ticket writer can cause a judge to throw it out.
* If you have the option—and the time—always fight a parking ticket in person. That way you can answer a judge's questions and clarify your argument.
* If you contest a parking ticket in person, be respectful

of the process. Dress nicely and never interrupt the judge.

* If you have to contest a ticket by mail, be as thorough as possible, and try to anticipate a judge's questions.

* When contesting a ticket by mail, attach all pictures and other evidence. It's better to have too many documents than too few.

* When dealing with a government agency, seek out the appropriate elected official.

* Elected officials fear losing votes, a fear you can and should take advantage of.

* If you have to visit a government agency, do so midweek, midmonth, and either midmorning or midafternoon to avoid long lines.

* Remember this mantra: I helped vote you into office, I can help vote you out, too.

10

MONEY BUSINESS
Holding Your Bank Accountable

It wasn't by choice that Kristine Hendon put her house up for sale. The mother of four had fallen on hard times and was desperate to avoid foreclosure. No longer able to afford her house payments, she asked her lender, Chase Home Financial, if it was willing to accept slightly less than she owed if she could find a potential buyer, a process known as a "short sale."

To her shock and delight, Chase agreed. The happy news didn't end there. Despite a housing market that was somewhere between ugly and atrocious, Hendon found a buyer. To top it all off, the sale went amazingly smoothly. On October 16, 2008, the title company cut Chase a check for $140,514.35, paying off what remained of her loan.

But when Hendon happened to check her credit report a year later, she just about had a stroke. Her house mortgage was still classified as "open," meaning Chase had not yet reported it as paid off. Hendon called the bank dozens of times, but could not get a straight answer about what was going on.

Hendon assumed it was a simple clerical error, but she was damned if she could get Chase to fix it. Months passed without resolution. Then, in early 2010, a Chase representative called her out of the blue. The woman informed Hendon matter-of-factly that she was a bit behind on her mortgage payments. With interest and penalties, the amount due came to . . . $43,000.

"I almost dropped the phone," Hendon said. "I'm like, are you kidding me?"

Sadly, Chase wasn't. Almost a year and a half after Hendon sold her house and paid off her mortgage, the bank still had not recorded the sale. She immediately faxed Chase documents proving the house was no longer hers and that she had repaid her debt, but the charges kept accruing.

"They just want to know where their money is," Hendon told me. "I said, 'Listen, I sold the home, I have papers that say the loan is closed. I have copies of the check. You guys cashed it. I have all these documents from my attorney and no one is telling me anything.'"

Don't you just love banks? Well, actually, you don't, according to a 2010 J.D. Power and Associates study. The report found that for the fourth consecutive year, customers' loyalty to banks declined, with more men and women saying they were considering switching their banks in the near future.

Why do we dislike our banks so much? Well, poor customer service doesn't help. Getting a problem resolved can be a little like breaking into Fort Knox. As Hendon found out, the folks on the front line at banks generally have little power to make major decisions. Banks, remember, live and die on one thing alone: money. They don't like to part with it easily.

The seemingly endless barrage of fees hasn't exactly helped banks endear themselves to customers either. I receive dozens of e-mails each month from angry bank customers whose checks have bounced, resulting in exorbitant fees.

In Hendon's case, it took her months to get her problem resolved. The major breakthrough came when her persistence got her bumped up the customer service food chain to someone in Chase's corporate offices. It took intervention at that level for someone at the bank to realize Hendon was right. The bank then erased the phantom $43,000 and contacted the credit bureaus and asked them to erase the debt. Ever the smart consumer, Hendon asked Chase to also put everything in writing, which resulted in a letter of apology that included a sentence in which Chase admitted it screwed up.

For Hendon, it would have been completely satisfying—if she hadn't just been through such bureaucratic hell.

"I'm still so angry with them," she told me later. "There were so many cooks in the kitchen, so to speak, that nobody knew what to do. They just kept handing me off to someone else. I was put under so much stress I actually had to go to the hospital a couple times. I had heart palpitations."

Banks will do that to you.

But you don't have to let them.

BATTLING THE BANK

If you feel you have been screwed over by a bank and it is unwilling to fix the problem, you have options. First, try to contact the bank, preferably by visiting your local branch and requesting to speak to the branch manager. Most times, the manager will fix the problem. If he or she doesn't, threaten to take your dispute to a higher level.

As is always the case when you're having a problem with a business, keep good notes. Write down when you visited, whom you spoke to, and what they said. Ask for bank employees to put what they're telling you in writing, creating a paper trail you can use later as you push your complaint up the food chain.

If your bank is a large financial institution, write a letter to the corporate offices. Again, the easiest way to find an address is to Google the bank's name and the words "corporate office address," or go to the bank's main website and look under "investor relations." If you're still having trouble finding an address, you can contact your bank's regulator (see page 130).

If you do get through to the corporate muckety-mucks, keep the response in your records. Push onward if you're not satisfied with the bank's response. Think of it as CSI: Banking. You're building a financial forensics case, so every piece of evidence is vital.

If you've struck out at every level, channel your unbridled anger by filing a complaint with the appropriate governing agency. In Hendon's case, she spent months battling Chase on her own, never realizing help was available. She never contacted the federal Office of the Comptroller of the Currency (the OCC), because she had no idea it existed.

"I didn't even know that was out there," she said. "I didn't even think about it, to be honest. I was just so frazzled."

I'm guessing she's not alone. Bank regulators aren't a particularly flashy group. They don't advertise, they're rarely quoted in the media, and with monikers like "the Office of the Comptroller of the Currency," their names don't exactly roll off the tongue.

"I agree there is an awareness issue," said Michael Stevens, senior vice president for regulatory policy for the Conference of State Bank Regulators. "The agencies have discussed it."

It's too bad these agencies aren't better known, because they can be important advocates in your fight against a bank. If you can prove your bank has wronged you, the regulating agency has the authority to investigate your claim. If the agency rules in your favor, it can force the bank to pay you restitution.

To file a complaint, you must first determine which agency regulates your bank. To do that, go to the Federal Financial Institutions Examination Council website at FFIEC.gov, then click on the "consumer help center" tab on the left. When the next screen pops up, click on "bank complaints or questions," and a search engine will appear, allowing you to enter the name of your bank. Type in the name and hit "search." A list will appear with your bank name and a link to the agency that regulates it.

You can conduct a similar search on the Federal Deposit Insurance Corporation's website at FDIC.gov. Click on the link labeled "bank find," then type in your bank's name. If you can't locate the "bank find" link, type "bank find" in the search space at the top of the main FDIC page. After entering your bank's name, information about the company will pop up, including the bank's main regulator.

There are several agencies working in this space. In some cases, more than one agency provides consumer protection for a bank. The previously mentioned Office of the Comptroller of the Currency (OCC.gov) regulates national banks. Generally speaking, national banks will have the word "national" in their names, or the letters "N.A." after their titles. The OCC has an incredibly comprehensive website that answers all kinds of questions about national banks at HelpWithMyBank.gov. In 2009, the OCC received roughly 72,000 complaints involving credit cards, mortgages, and checking accounts.

"We look into the complaint and contact the bank and keep the customer informed about what we're doing," said Dean De-Buck, a spokesman for the agency. "We'll find out what the story is. If something needs to be corrected, we'll take it from there."

The agency even allows you to appeal its ruling if you're not happy with it. In fact, if you're not happy with the results of the appeal, you can appeal the appeal, giving you, in effect, three chances to win.

If your bank is state-chartered, you can file a complaint with the FDIC or with your state's banking regulator. To find your state regulator, go to the Conference of State Bank Supervisors website at CSBS.org. Click on "about us," and search for "state banking departments." A list will pop up with contact information for bank regulators in all fifty states. All state agencies have a method by which you can file a complaint.

The Office of Thrift Supervision (www.ots.treas.gov) regulates federal savings and loans and federal savings banks, and the National Credit Union Administration (NCUA.gov) oversees federally chartered credit unions. (See the appendix for help determining if your credit union is state or federally chartered.)

All of the aforementioned agencies have staffs dedicated to investigating your complaints, and all have easy-to-fill-out complaint forms available on their websites. If you've done your homework, taken good notes, and kept copies of all relevant documents, filling out a complaint form likely won't take more than ten or fifteen minutes.

The investigating agency will acknowledge receipt of your complaint within days, in most cases. It might also give you a reference number for your files. Make sure you keep that number. It can take several weeks (sometimes a few months, depending on the complexity of your case) for the agency to investigate your complaint, but you will get an answer.

"If you feel you're having trouble getting a response from your bank, I can guarantee your regulator will not have trouble," Stevens said. "From a consumer standpoint, at least you have someone out there to make a judgment about whether the financial institution was right or wrong."

Sometimes, just getting your bank to listen is all it takes. Darcie Verhaeghe had the unfortunate circumstance of battling not one, but two banks. Months earlier, she made an online payment from her Chase checking account to her Bank of America credit card. The $1,281.70 was successfully deducted from her Chase account, but it was never credited to her Bank of America credit card.

Try as she might, Verhaeghe could not convince the two banks that her money was lost.

"Every time I call, they claim they are going to investigate the missing payment," she told me.

Three months later, the $1,281.70 was still nowhere to be

found. It was as if some magic bank fairy had flittered off with her money. It seemed the banks weren't particularly thrilled about the prospect of going on a magic-fairy hunt.

It took Verhaeghe more than a dozen calls, but she finally broke through the previously impenetrable bank barrier: she was able to get representatives from both banks on the phone at the same time in a three-way call. Once the banks actually talked to each other, they were able to locate the missing money within minutes. Turned out, the $1,281.70 had mistakenly been routed to Bank of America's home-mortgage division, where it sat untouched for months.

Verhaeghe raised such a ruckus, Bank of America not only transferred the money to the appropriate account, it gave her a $100 Best Buy gift card for her troubles.

Prior to the three-way call, both banks moved with all the urgency of a three-toed sloth.

"I could never get anyone to give me an answer at Bank of America," Verhaeghe said. "When I called, they all acted like I was crazy."

She was, of course, far from crazy. Like I said, banks can do this to you.

Sometimes, your best approach is to fight fire with fire. Remember, it's your money, so you have the power, not the bank. If a bank only loves you for your assets, reserve any reciprocal adoration for a financial institution that treats you with respect.

Despite the recent rash of bank failures, there is still plenty of competition among financial institutions, all of which would love to store your money. There's a reason banks offer all kinds of crazy incentives if you set up an account. They're not just giving you a free iPod or $100 cash out of the kindness of their hearts. They know they'll make back their token investment and much more from your money. Losing you as a customer means the bank is losing what it likes about you the most—your assets. It's never a bad idea to remind a bank that your loyalty has a price.

If you're not getting results, threaten to leave. If you still don't get results, take your money and go.

"I think we've all been there and experienced that frustration in one form or another," said Greg McBride, a senior financial analyst at Bankrate.com. "As consumers, we are free agents. We can shop around and take our business elsewhere."

If you're dealing with a larger institution and you're finding it difficult to speak to a human being, consider changing to a smaller, community bank. As long as your deposits are FDIC insured, you don't have to worry about whether the bank fails, meaning your smaller, local bank might be a better fit. McBride said smaller banks are often more responsive, in large part because they know it's the only way they can compete with the bigger national institutions.

"There are smaller banks and credit unions that are very focused on customer satisfaction for that very reason," McBride said. "They're very happy to take in the customers of unresponsive larger banks. Vote with your feet."

THE THREE-WAY

Darcie Verhaeghe got nowhere in her bank fight until she was able to get representatives from both Chase and Bank of America on the line at the same time.

I've spoken to customer service experts at many large companies who are instructed not to engage in three-way calls, but sometimes if you push them hard enough, they will consent.

To request a three-way call between two companies, try first to get the name and phone number for a customer service representative at each company. Ask both representatives if they will consent to a three-way call. If one agrees but the other doesn't, ask the agreeing representative to initiate the call.

Getting all interested parties on the line together can eliminate hours of frustration and cut through red tape quickly. It never hurts to try.

REMEMBER:

* If you have a problem with your bank, first visit your local branch and ask to speak to the manager.
* Keep detailed notes with dates, times, locations, and names.
* Write the bank's president.

* File a complaint with your bank's regulating agency.
* To find your bank's regulator, visit FFIEC.gov.
* If you don't like the regulator's ruling, file an appeal. Most regulators will let you.
* If you still can't get results, threaten to take your money to another bank.
* Switch to a small, community bank if you're disgruntled with your large, impersonal one.
* If you switch, make sure your new bank is FDIC insured.

11

CREDIT CRUNCH
Getting a Handle on Your History

It's amazing the things you'll put up with when you're young. When my wife and I first moved to Chicago, we were so desperate to find a reasonably priced apartment in a nice neighborhood that we settled for the first decent-looking place with a FOR RENT sign in the window.

The apartment, which comprised the top floor of the landlord's house, was heated by two large gas stoves. They were not what you would call efficient.

Although it was advertised as a two-bedroom apartment, the second room was barely big enough to fit our twin-sized futon. The so-called "master" bedroom wasn't much larger. To house our queen bed, we had to wedge the mattress and box spring into one end of the room, where it was bordered on three sides by the bedroom's walls. If I wanted to go to the bathroom in the middle of the night, I had to climb over my sleeping wife. The water pressure in the shower was so weak I sometimes left for work with bubbles from my Head & Shoulders still fizzing in my ears. The hardwood floors crackled, the refrigerator sounded like it was revving up to take flight, and on windy days the front door leading to the stairs below would fly open with such force, you'd swear the entire house was about to crumble.

But as bad as all that was, the worst part by far was the creaking from the attic every night around 3 a.m. I have no earthly idea what was going on up there. I'm still convinced the place was haunted (my wife, the only sane one in the family, has some more plausible ideas, but I choose not to believe them).

Whatever the cause—whether the house was built on an ancient Indian burial ground (my theory) or the landlord did odd woodworking projects in the dead of night (my wife's theory—yeah, right), we were more than ready to set out on our own after a year of cold, creepy, bladder-busting nights.

We were a bit more methodical in our search for a condo. We made a list of everything we absolutely needed, like a garage space, a patio, a good view, and a modern kitchen. We promptly fell in love with a loft that had none of those things. Still, it was sharp, modern, and seemingly ghost-free.

It was with great pride and trepidation that we began the process of buying our first place. The whole process made us nervous. The down payment ate up our entire savings. We had never purchased anything even remotely as expensive.

It took us weeks to navigate the process—finding an inspector, gathering our documents, crunching the numbers. We thought we had finally gotten all our ducks in a row when the mortgage broker called with some bad news: she had pulled our credit reports and found a bit of a surprise. My wife's credit was spotless. Mine—not so much.

Years earlier, when I was fresh out of college and dirt poor, I had an emergency appendectomy. Luckily, I had health insurance at the time. Unluckily, that health insurance sucked.

Turned out, I still owed one of the doctors $231. For what, I have no idea. It was, to say the least, an unpleasant blast from the past. If I had ever known about the debt, I had long since erased it from my memory. The credit bureaus, it seems, have slightly better recall.

Because I had such a small credit history, the unpaid $231 was dragging down my credit score. And a less-than-pristine credit score meant a slightly higher mortgage rate.

It was my first crash course in the murky and sometimes scary world of credit.

Few documents have a greater impact on our lives than our credit reports, and few numbers define us as importantly as our credit scores. At some point in our lives, most of us will have to take out a car loan or a house mortgage or apply for a credit card. All of those transactions are impacted by your credit history. Heck, even your landlord or potential employers can check your credit report as part of a background check.

It all makes knowing your credit history—and fixing mistakes on your credit report—vitally important. If I had been on the ball a decade ago when I was buying my first condo, I would have checked my credit report weeks or months before I went looking for a mortgage. I would have saved myself a huge surprise, and I might have been able to remove the doctor's charges (if they had been reported erroneously) before the mortgage companies took a gander at my reports.

Thankfully, keeping track of your credit history is not difficult. Federal law mandates you be allowed one free copy of your credit report every year from each of the three credit bureaus—Equifax, TransUnion, and Experian. Some states (Colorado, Georgia, Maine, Maryland, Massachusetts, New Jersey, and Vermont) have laws allowing you more free copies. Take full advantage.

To receive your free credit report, go to AnnualCreditReport.com or call 877-322-8228. While many websites and commercials advertise "free" reports, www.AnnualCreditReport.com is the only official site for obtaining the reports. Most of the other sites are actually businesses that wind up charging you for their services. Avoid them.

It's a relatively simple process. It took me less than five minutes to obtain a copy of my credit report in a recent attempt. After typing in some identifying information (my name, address, and Social Security number) I was asked a few questions (the amount of my last mortgage payment, the name of a bank where I had taken out a loan). Moments later, my TransUnion credit report popped up.

What was on there? A lot, actually. There was a payment history for every credit card I've ever owned, along with a history of my car and mortgage payments. There was even a history of my payments to the gas company. In each case, the report showed all of my payments for the past four years, along with notations about whether I paid on time or late—and how late.

It showed my remaining balances and outstanding debts. It was actually a bit scary. The report laid out my whole financial life before me. I scanned it thoroughly to look for errors. Thankfully, there were none. But mistakes happen, and more frequently than you might think.

In my job as the Problem Solver, I've received dozens—perhaps hundreds—of e-mails from folks whose credit histories are pockmarked with erroneously reported debts. Most of the folks I hear from had not checked their credit reports regularly, and were unpleasantly surprised (as I was a decade ago) when they went to take out a new loan.

Because you're entitled to one free report annually from each of the three credit bureaus, you can actually get three reports every year. While the reports from each bureau will vary slightly, all three are basically the same. Most major credit card companies, mortgage lenders, and banks will report to all the three bureaus simultaneously. What does that mean for you? Well, to monitor your credit history throughout the year, you can spread out your free credit report requests through www.AnnualCreditReport.com. For instance, you can request a free report from TransUnion in January, a report from Experian in May, and a report from Equifax in September. That way, you only go about four months between checks.

If you spot an error, it's imperative that you begin fixing it immediately. The longer it lingers on your credit report, the more difficult it can be to remove it.

I once received an e-mail from a man named Lee Duncan. He had recently gone to refinance the mortgage on his house, but when the lender pulled his credit history, there was an unpaid bill from American Express. Duncan was flabbergasted. He had spoken to American Express months earlier about the charge, which was made in error. The credit card company had promised to remove the charge and not report it to the credit agencies.

But there it was.

It was not a minor issue. The blemish lowered his credit score, so the bank tacked on 2.5 points to his refinanced mortgage. The cost to Duncan: an additional $8,000.

Because his credit report was incorrect, he had to forgo the refinancing. He wasn't willing to pay the extra $8,000 for a lower rate. At first he was peeved. Then he went to work to get his credit reports fixed.

How did he do it? All three credit bureaus included the error on their credit reports, so Duncan filed a dispute with each of them. Dispute forms are available from each of the bureaus' websites. When filing a dispute, write down exactly what is inaccurate in the report.

Include copies of supporting documents, such as a paid bill, or, if it's a case of mistaken identity, proof that the unpaid bill belongs to someone else. Keep copies of everything you send, then ship the dispute letter by certified mail with a return receipt requested. That way, you have proof the credit bureau has received it.

"The credit agencies have a duty under the law to investigate," said Ira Reingold, executive director of the National Association of Consumer Advocates. "The problem is they take your complaint letter, turn it into an electronic code, and send it to the business you're disputing. Often, the business will respond saying, 'No, it's him.' Then the credit reporting agency says, 'No, it's you.'"

To try to avoid such problems, you should also contact the

company that reported the debt. It's often easier to deal directly with the bank or the business that's involved than it is with a credit bureau. At the very least, it might be easier to talk to someone in person or over the phone, allowing you to explain why the debt was reported in error. The company can then contact the credit bureaus and correct the mistake quickly.

Once you've filed a dispute with a credit bureau, it has thirty days to investigate your claim. If you plan to take out a loan in the next month or two, pull your credit reports early so you have time to complete the dispute process before the transaction is made. If you have already used up your free reports for the year, you can still pay to receive a new one. They generally cost around $10 a copy, a small price to pay for peace of mind.

It's not just billing errors that can show up on your credit report. Another reader once wrote me because her Equifax report showed she had no credit history at all. None of her credit cards were on there. Neither were her home or auto loans. If you think it's difficult to get a good loan with a blemish on your credit report, try getting one with no report at all. Lenders aren't superenthused about handing you money when you have no history of payments.

Turned out, the woman's first name, Limo, had tripped up Equifax's system. The credit bureau's computers screened out the word "limousine"—and all its derivations. The computer assumed she was a car, not a person, and rejected all incoming information about her credit history.

The lesson isn't that you should avoid naming your kids after vehicles (Mercedes is a beautiful name, and Chevy Chase has had a long and fine career), but rather that credit bureaus are far from perfect. It's important to stay on top of them.

After you file a dispute, the credit bureau will send you a letter with its findings. If it rules against you and you still think it's wrong, you can attach a "consumer statement" to your credit report explaining your side. You get up to a hundred words, which isn't much, but your note will be seen by potential lenders.

Of course, if the debt on your credit report is accurate, you can file as many disputes as you want—the blemish isn't coming off anytime soon.

"Your credit report does follow you," said Catherine Williams, vice president of financial literacy for Money Management International, a nonprofit credit counseling organization.

HOW BAD CAN IT BE?

Ultimately, what does one missed payment mean for you? There are no hard-and-fast rules about how each debt will affect your credit history. Before granting you a loan, most lenders will obtain your credit score, which is basically a reflection of the items on your credit report. If you think of your credit report as a library of your credit history, your credit score is like a book review.

The most commonly used credit score is called FICO, which is short for Fair Isaac Corporation, the company that provides the score. In general, the score is calculated by weighing five factors: your payment history, how much you owe on each account, your length of credit history, your new credit, and your types of credit.

Trying to make heads or tails out of all that can be maddening. In reality, the formula FICO uses is a bit like the recipe for Coke—it's never completely spelled out. If you want to find out more about the components that make up your FICO score, check out www.myfico.com.

Although the scores range from 300 to 850, most fall within the 600 to 750 range. The higher the score, the better your chance to get a loan—and at a better rate.

If you have legitimate debts and missed payments on your credit report, there are no quick fixes. Many companies advertise that they can fix your credit report and improve your credit score. Avoid them. In almost every case, these companies are scam artists, pure and simple. They take your money and give you nothing.

The truth is, the only way to fix a damaged credit report is to pay off all debts, then continue making timely payments on all of your bills.

"Your score will heal over time," Williams said.

If you have only minor issues on your credit report, Williams said, your credit score can rebound in about a year. If you file for bankruptcy, it can stay on your credit report for up to a decade.

"Making regular, on-time payments is the most important thing to keeping a good credit score," Williams said. "I'm going to have that engraved on my tombstone."

That's thinking ahead.

As for Duncan, he was able to correct the error with all three of the credit reporting agencies, although he says that the experience was "pretty much ridiculous."

In the end, he had to check with Experian, Equifax, and TransUnion, along with American Express, repeatedly. American Express had to write two letters to Equifax explaining what had happened and why the debt should be erased. But it worked.

What did he learn, other than dogged determination wins out? He learned how powerful the credit bureaus can be, and just how important it is to keep close tabs on his credit history.

"So much of what we do is controlled by our credit score," he said. "These companies have so much power over us, especially in the economy we're living in."

True, true.

As for me, the house I currently live in is toasty warm in the winter, and appears to be completely ghost free. I've even exorcised the ghosts of my financial past. I'm happy to report the delinquent $231 doctor payment has now been purged from my credit report. Time, in fact, does heal old credit wounds.

REMEMBER:

* Federal law mandates that you can receive one free credit report each year from each of the three major credit bureaus. Take full advantage.
* You can spread out your free reports over the course

of the year by requesting one report from a different credit bureau every four months.

* If you plan to make a major purchase or take out a loan, pull your credit report at least a month earlier, so you have time to fix any mistakes.
* If you find an error in your credit history, report it immediately.
* To file a dispute, go to the credit bureau's website or call the bureau's dispute phone number.
* Send in your dispute via certified mail.
* Always contact the company that reported your debt and try to resolve the issue there first. If the company made an error, it can remove the notation from your credit report.
* If the credit bureau rules against you in its investigation, you can write a hundred-word "consumer statement" that it will attach to your credit report, explaining your side of the matter.
* There are no "quick fixes" to repair your credit report or improve your credit score.
* Avoid companies that make grand promises to improve your credit score immediately.

12

STOP, THIEF
Protecting Your Identity

Jean Santschi never saw the men who stole her wallet, but she knows they had their eyes on her. Since it happened, the eighty-two-year-old has replayed the incident over and over in her head. The best she can figure is that the thieves picked her out as soon as she set foot in the grocery store, then followed her up and down the aisles, waiting for their chance.

When they struck, they struck quickly. Santschi had placed her purse in the seat of the grocery cart. By her estimation, it was out of her sight for only a few seconds, just long enough for her to grab some cans off the shelf.

When she returned to the cart and reached into the purse to change her glasses, she noticed immediately it was lighter. She fished around for her wallet and realized it was gone.

"They were professionals," Santschi said. "They were waiting for me to make a mistake and I did. I turned around."

In a panic, she made a beeline to the store's customer service counter. She asked for the manager, but the woman behind the counter seemed stuck in molasses. After a few anxious moments, Santschi decided she couldn't take it anymore. Leaving her groceries in her cart, she retrieved her car from the parking lot and drove to the local police station.

"I was a nervous wreck," she said. "I said, 'Someone has just stolen my wallet.'"

She called her husband and told him to contact all her credit card companies. It was no easy task. Santschi's wallet contained almost a dozen cards, including cards from American Express, Citibank, Discover, three gas station chains, and handful of department stores.

Despite her lightning-fast response, the thieves were already at work. As her husband methodically worked his way down the list of credit cards, the men who stole her wallet had already visited Kmart, Home Depot, and several gas stations, racking up almost $1,000 in charges.

She was able to get the charges erased. That part was relatively easy. Under the federal Fair Credit Billing Act, a consumer is only responsible for up to $50 in unauthorized charges on a credit card. All of the credit card companies erased the entire amount the thieves had charged, including the allowable $50.

Ensuring her identity wasn't stolen for other purposes was a bit more difficult. In the previous chapter, we looked at the importance of credit bureaus and how to deal with them. Never is that information more important than after your identity has been stolen.

Not all identity theft is the same. Some cases are much easier to deal with than others. As mentioned above, if someone has used your credit card number to make an unwarranted purchase, you're covered under the Fair Credit Billing Act. Often, a simple call to the credit card company is all it takes to get the charge wiped clean. Depending on the charge and the credit card company, you might be asked to fill out an affidavit. If so, do it immediately. The longer you wait to file your paperwork the more cumbersome the process becomes.

The key is identifying problems as quickly as possible. At the risk of sounding like a broken record, I'll make this point again: check your monthly statements religiously. I'm a little paranoid (this job will do that to you), but I check my credit card and checking accounts several times a week online. It might sound obsessive, but it can make a difference. One morning, I logged on and saw that someone had charged $1,400 worth of luggage on my credit card.

At 3 a.m. central standard time.

In Indonesia.

Given the relative confines of the time-space continuum, along with my absolute ambivalence toward high-priced suitcases *and* the fact that I was comfortably asleep in my bed in Chicago at the time, I was pretty sure that wasn't me in Jakarta charging up a Samsonite storm.

I called Visa, which immediately erased the charges—no affidavit required. The customer service agent canceled my card and sent me a new one, which arrived a few days later. Truth be told, it was a pain in the butt. I had to contact every business that was making automatic deductions from my Visa account and give them my new account number.

But the quick response was worth it. If I had waited, the person who had my credit card number could have continued charging items to my account, which, at the very least, would have made the dispute process a tad more tedious. More important, the clock was ticking. Under federal law, you have only sixty days to report an erroneous charge. After that, you're out of luck.

Disputing bogus credit card charges is child's play. Things get a bit more challenging if your identity has been used in other ways.

If someone applies for credit in your name but uses another address, you might not know about it until it pops up on your credit report, or when you receive a collection notice. Worse yet, you could hear about it because you're named in a lawsuit. All the more reason to pull your free credit reports a couple of times a year.

In most cases, if your credit card account has been used fraudulently but there is no evidence your Social Security number has been obtained, there is no need to request a fraud alert, which can make opening new lines of credit much more arduous. In the worst-case scenario, if someone has obtained your Social Security number and opened credit accounts in your name, the mess can be difficult to untangle.

The first thing you want to do is call the credit bureaus and place a fraud alert on your account. Although the three bureaus (Exeprian, TransUnion, and Equifax) are required by law to forward your information to the other two agencies, I've heard from readers who say that doesn't always happen. If you're a victim of credit fraud, it's best to contact all three bureaus individually. The way I see it, you're better off knowing the information has reached all of its intended targets.

The initial fraud alert stays on your credit report for ninety days. During that time, a business cannot issue you credit without first verifying your identity. Often, that means calling you directly, so make sure the credit bureau has your cell phone number or another way to contact you quickly. The idea of the fraud alert is to prevent thieves from opening new accounts without your knowledge.

Mari Frank, who wrote the book on identity theft (two of them, actually), suggests going even further and asking for an extended fraud alert, which stays on your account for seven years. To receive an extended alert, you are required to obtain a theft report from a law enforcement agency—often your local police department, your state's attorney general's office, or even the postal authority. You can also file a report with the Federal Trade Commission, at www.ftc.gov/idtheft. The FTC sometimes refers your complaint to other government agencies that can provide help.

Most states also have laws that allow you to place a security freeze on your credit. That way, potential creditors cannot gain access to your credit report unless you temporarily lift the freeze. The freeze, which usually costs about $10 per credit bureau to enable or lift, creates a huge barrier for potential fraudsters. But it can also make it more cumbersome for you to obtain new credit. Before opting for a freeze, decide if you're soon going to apply for a new credit card or loan. If so, you might want to consider sticking with the plain old fraud alert.

Once you've dealt with the credit bureaus, you can begin the process of contacting your bank, credit card companies, and other agencies that might have been impacted by your stolen identity, including utilities. Change account numbers if they have been compromised, along with your PIN numbers and security passwords. If you think your Social Security number has been used, contact the Social Security Administration immediately.

Frank, a victim of identity theft herself, said it can take years to unravel the mess caused by an identity thief.

The good news is, with hard work and some patience, it can be done. The bad news is, there is absolutely no way to completely protect yourself from having your identity stolen.

Evan Hendricks, editor and publisher of *Privacy Times*, a Maryland-based privacy-issues newsletter, said your personal information is so widely dispersed, it is impossible to control it completely.

"You can do everything right and still have your information compromised," he said.

The numbers are downright scary. According to a report by Javelin Strategy & Research, 11.1 million U.S. adults were victims of identity theft in 2009, an increase of 12 percent over 2008, and a 37 percent increase over 2007.

WHAT CAN YOU DO TO STAY SAFE?

Although there is no guarantee you won't be victimized, there are some simple things you can do to decrease the odds—or at least make things a tad more difficult for conniving thieves.

First and foremost, protect your Social Security number. For con artists it is the skeleton key, a nine-digit code that can unlock your identity and allow unscrupulous interlopers to set up accounts in your name. Never carry your Social Security card in your purse or wallet. If your purse is lost or stolen, as was the case with Santschi, your Social Security number can quickly find its way into the hands of someone with less-than-honorable intentions.

Hendricks said there are only a handful of institutions to which you are legally required to hand over your Social Security number. You must give it to your employer for wage and tax purposes. You must also give it to your bank so it can report interest payments to the IRS. Many governmental agencies will also request the number.

Other than that, Hendricks advises being stingy with it. Many companies and utilities will request it because it provides the easiest way to trace someone who doesn't pay their debts, or pull a credit report.

"It's just a valuable piece of information," Hendricks said.

Doctors' offices, for instance, routinely ask for your Social Security number.

"I never give it because it's not required by law," Hendricks said. "Most of the time they don't come back and badger me for it. I have health insurance, so they don't really need my Social Security number."

If a company or agency refuses to deal with you unless you provide the number, you can either take your business elsewhere, or take a stand. Sometimes the business will relent, other times it won't. Generally, you have other options, so if you're uncomfortable giving your Social Security number to someone, don't do it.

If your health insurance company uses your Social Security number as your ID number, ask for a substitute number.

If you shop online, make sure your computer is protected. Install antivirus and anti-spyware programs and keep them updated. You can also install a personal firewall, which protects your computer from hackers, Internet worms, and viruses.

When you pay for something online, always use a credit card, which allows you to dispute a charge if your account number becomes compromised. In fact, Frank advises using a credit card for virtually every purchase. Debit cards and checking accounts are not protected by the Fair Credit Billing Act, so if someone steals those account numbers, it can be difficult, and sometimes impossible, to get your money back.

If you do use your credit card online, make sure the website is secure. Look for an "s" (which stands for "secure") at the beginning or the end of the "http" coding on the website's address and a padlock symbol somewhere in the web browser (it's often at the bottom of the browser or next to the web address field).

"Otherwise, anyone can go in and grab it," said Jennifer Leach of OnGuardOnline.gov, a Federal Trade Commission website.

Never give your personal information via e-mail or on a cell phone, which are not secure. If you're asked to create a password, especially for an Internet account that contains sensitive information like your bank account or credit card number, make it a tough one. The longer the password, the tougher it is to crack. A ten-character password is better than one with only eight. Adding a combination of letters, numbers, and symbols helps as well. Do not, under any circumstance, include your name or address in a password. For instance, Jonyates1969 is much easier for thieves to crack than, say, dingbat$29boo. Please note, however, that "dingbat$29boo" is *not* my password for anything. I swear it.

Even if it were, it wouldn't be for long. It's always good to change your passwords regularly. The FTC recommends changing them every three months. Use different passwords for different accounts. That way, if a thief decodes one of your passwords, he or she hasn't gained access to all of your accounts. Although the various passwords might be difficult to remember, never leave a list of them in a public place, like at work if you share a computer. You can always reset a specific password if you forget it.

When you're done with your computer, turn it off. Leaving your computer on all day and all night is like a dream come true for scammers, who can remotely install malicious software on your machine, then control it for their own devious reasons.

"The bad guys are really good at what they do," Leach said. "It's their job to get you to give them money."

And it's your job to make sure you don't. Never provide personal information to anyone who e-mails, calls, or writes asking for bank account numbers, your Social Security number, or credit card information. If you don't know exactly who you're dealing with, it is likely a scam. If the e-mail or letter claims to be from a bank or an institution you do business with, find a number independently for the business, then call and ask if it has, in fact, requested the information.

If you have copies of utility bills, credit card bills, or other

paperwork that includes account numbers or sensitive information, shred the paper before throwing it out. Once your trash
leaves your house, you have no control over who sees it.

Stan Ciesla, a former garbage industry employee, once
told me most people would be shocked at how easy it is for
thieves to sort through your trash.

"People would get their monthly IRA statements—there'd
be a half a million dollars on there. They'd read them and
just throw them in the garbage," Ciesla said. "That's the worst
thing you can do. It was brutal. People didn't care."

Ciesla saw it happen so often, he decided to quit the garbage business and start his own company: Beaver Shredding,
Inc. Business, he said, is booming. But you don't need to pay
someone else to dispose of your sensitive documents. A cheap
paper shredder can pay for itself with a single shredding.

Of course in Santschi's case, it was a pickpocket who did
her in. The theft might have been simple, but the damage was
complex. It took her months to straighten everything out.

Police caught the thieves, using surveillance tapes from the
Kmart to catch them in the act of using one of her credit cards.
Another camera caught them leaving the store and jumping
into their car—capturing the license plate in the process. Santschi said she was told one of the men served jail time. The other
provided evidence that helped detectives nab a more important
suspect.

More than a year later, she still checks her credit report
regularly. So far, she has seen no new evidence of her identity
being used for other purposes.

What did she learn from the experience?

"You have to be very vigilant," Santschi said.

You also have to be smart. She no longer signs the back of her credit cards, which forces cashiers to ask for her ID before processing a charge.

It's a pain in the butt, she said, but it's worth it.

"We are more cautious now," she said. "I'm glad it's over."

REMEMBER:

* Under the Fair Credit Billing Act, you are only responsible for the first $50 of unauthorized charges on your credit card.
* The law gives you sixty days to report an erroneous credit card charge.
* If your identity has been stolen, call the credit bureaus immediately and place a fraud alert on your credit report.
* A fraud alert lasts ninety days. During that time, no business can open or close a credit account in your name without calling you for your approval.
* You can also request an extended fraud alert, which lasts seven years. For that, you must obtain a police report.
* For about $10, you can place a credit freeze on your accounts. Under a freeze, no business can issue you credit unless you temporarily lift the barrier.

* If your identity has been stolen, change account numbers and passwords.
* Be stingy with your Social Security number. Only give it out if absolutely necessary.
* Install antivirus and anti-spyware programs on your computer and keep them updated.
* If you shop online, always use a credit card, and make sure the website has an "s" at the beginning or end of the "http" coding on the website's address, and a padlock symbol somewhere in the web browser (usually at the bottom or next to the web address field).
* Make your passwords long and intricate, and change them often.
* When you're done with bills, statements, and other sensitive documents, shred them.

13

CAR TALK
Keeping Dealers and Mechanics Honest

As I drove to the car dealership with my colleague and column partner, Kristin Samuelson, in the passenger seat, she confided in me that she was a little scared. Her last trip to a car dealer hadn't gone particularly well.

"I literally had a panic attack the night before I went," Samuelson said. "I had a meltdown. I was crying. I thought I was going to walk in and get taken advantage of. I thought I'd get myself in too deep with payments. I mean, buying a car is the second biggest purchase you can make, after buying a house."

Now before I go on, let me categorically state that Samuelson is no shrinking violet. She's tough as nails, yet the thought of buying a car stressed her out so much, she was driven to tears. Part of the reason she was anxious was because her last attempt had gone so poorly.

She was so unprepared, she became flustered. She had no idea what kind of car she wanted, or what she wanted to pay for it. After a round of fruitless negotiations, she simply gave up.

Still haunted by that experience, Samuelson asked me to go along as she went car shopping to find a replacement for her Malibu. She needed support. She needed a sounding board.

She needed an extra BS detector to make sure she didn't get swindled by a smooth-talking car salesman.

I was more than happy to oblige.

"I think they treat women differently," she said. "And I don't really know much about cars at all."

Most of us don't. And she was right—buying a car *is* one of life's most important investments. Buy a bad one and you're stuck with an endless string of repair bills. Pay too much, and you're stuck with a checkbook-draining car payment.

The good news is that these days, there are more tools than ever to help you navigate the potential minefield that is a car sales lot.

Most important, never go shopping for a new or used car unprepared. Samuelson's first trip to a car dealership was a disaster because, among other things, she did virtually no research beforehand.

"Looking back at it, I was a total idiot," she admitted as we drove down Interstate 55 toward a Honda dealership on Chicago's Southwest Side. "I thought the only thing you could do was talk them down from the sticker price. I didn't even look up the invoice price."

Ah, but she learned. Before our trip to the Honda lot, Samuelson spent some time on the Internet, first looking at different makes and models. After some research, she decided she wanted a Honda, preferably a Civic.

She went to Kelley Blue Book's website, KBB.com, which lists all cars and models, along with their manufacturer's suggested retail price, or MSRP, the price set by the manufacturer. It also lists the car's invoice cost—or the amount a dealer pays for the car—and the average price customers have paid for it.

She then went to Edmunds.com, which provides its own list of prices, along with a list of "incentives" the manufacturer is offering on the car. Samuelson discovered that Honda was offering 1.9 percent financing, and that it was giving its dealers $1,000 in "dealer cash"—basically an extra $1,000 it could take off the price in an effort to sell the car.

Edmunds.com also lists car companies' "dealer holdback" numbers, which is a percentage of the MSRP or invoice price that the manufacturer holds on to and then repays the dealer later. The practice, which started several years ago, often allows dealers the ability to sell a car at the invoice price but still make a profit. Edmunds listed Honda's dealer holdback as 2 percent of the vehicle's base MSRP. It's a good fact to know in case the salesman gets all teary-eyed and claims he or she can't make a profit selling you a car for less than the sticker price.

Armed with the numbers and information, she knew what she could expect to pay for a new Civic. She knew at what point the dealer would probably break even, and had a pretty good idea whether a dealer's counteroffer would be genuine or an attempt to take advantage of her.

"This is one product where it's pretty easy to figure out what you should pay," said Jack Nerad, executive editorial director for Kelley Blue Book. "You can't just walk into Sears knowing what a refrigerator cost the store to stock, but you can walk into a Honda dealer or a Chevy dealer knowing what the dealer paid for the car."

Samuelson was armed with much more than just that. She also printed out a copy of her credit report, so there were no surprises when she got to the dealership. If you agree on a car, the dealer will do its own check of your credit, so it's best to know what's on your report before going in. The report affects not only your ability to obtain a car loan but your rate.

If you're serious about buying a car, shop around for loans at your bank and other lenders before you arrive at the dealership. Philip Reed, senior consumer-advice editor at Edmunds.com, suggests getting a preapproved loan as a defense against potential salesmen shenanigans. By obtaining a signed loan offer from an outside creditor, you have a bargaining chip when you go to negotiate your car purchase. In one classic ploy, the salesman will ask you how much you can afford to pay per month on a car loan. If you say $300, the salesman might try to convince you that you can pay more, or add features and financing terms that needlessly tack on money until it reaches your stated maximum.

If you arrive armed with a preapproved loan, you can tell the dealer you intend to pay with cash. The dealership might counter with a better financing plan. In Samuelson's case, the offer of 1.9 percent financing was much better than the terms of any loan she could get from another bank. If that happens, by all means take the car dealership's loan offer. If the dealership's loan terms are worse than your preapproved offer, you've already secured yourself the best deal possible.

"People focus on 'I'm going to go in there and beat these guys up and get a good price,'" Reed said. "But financing it correctly is, in the big picture, going to save you more money."

RUNNING THE NUMBERS

A $15,000 loan financed at 7 percent over five years will cost you just $297 a month, which might sound good. But over the course of the loan, you'll pay a whopping $2,820 in interest. A shorter-term loan at a better rate, say 3 percent over four years, will cost you another $35 a month. But you'll spend less than $1,000 in interest—a savings of more than $1,800 compared to the loan with the higher interest rate.

Rate	Years/months	Monthly payment	Total payment	Total interest paid
2%	3 Yrs/36 months	$429.64	$15,467.04	$467.04
	4 Yrs/48 months	$325.43	$15,620.64	$620.64
	5 Yrs/60 months	$262.92	$15,775.20	$775.20
5%	3 Yrs/36 months	$449.56	$16,184.16	$1,184.16
	4 Yrs/48 months	$345.44	$16,581.12	$1,581.12
	5 Yrs/60 months	$283.07	$16,984.20	$1,984.20
10%	3 Yrs/36 months	$484.01	$17,424.36	$2,424.36
	4 Yrs/48 months	$380.44	$18,261.12	$3,261.12
	5 Yrs/60 months	$318.71	$19,122.60	$4,122.60

Armed with all of this information, Samuelson and I entered the dealership's showroom with a certain swagger. We weren't cocky, just confident we knew enough to avoid getting taken. The door hadn't even closed behind us before a salesman named José shook our hands and introduced himself. He was pleasant enough, but he spoke a million miles a minute, rattling off horsepower, mileage, and obscure features of each model on the showroom floor. Perhaps the constant repetition of reciting the same spiel, multiple times a day, had engrained the words in his head. Either way, it was both impressive and slightly intimidating, like having our own personal Rain Man.

We sat in two cars, then an SUV, and finally a minivan. Throughout, José remained calm and low pressure. He told us of the deals that were available, and seemed content letting us go at our own pace. After about forty-five minutes, when we were done looking, José took us over to his cubicle to get Samuelson's information. As we were about to leave, he excused himself and walked away for a few minutes.

Then the games started. He returned with his boss who was, shall we say, a tad less laid back. He practically insisted Samuelson test-drive a car. Samuelson politely declined. He told her it was imperative. She again said no. We began to get a bad feeling about the whole experience.

Sure enough, José's boss asked Samuelson how much she could pay per month. When she said she was uncomfortable saying and that she wasn't ready to buy a car that day, he applied a full-court press. He told her she had to act quickly or the incentives on the car would expire. He tried to imply that if she didn't buy a car immediately, she'd be screwed. Although her old car had almost died and she desperately needed a new one, Samuelson did not panic.

In my mind, I heard the words of Nerad from Kelley Blue

Book, who had warned me that salesmen are taught to complete the sale that day, and that if a potential buyer leaves the lot, he or she likely will never come back.

"Because the market is so hotly competitive, your best negotiating tool is your feet, and by that I mean if you hear something you don't like, if you're just uncomfortable for any reason, get up and walk out," Nerad told me. "You're going to find just as good a deal the next day or the day after that."

So we left the dealership carless, but with a better understanding of exactly what she wanted—and how much she would probably have to spend. She also knew she did *not* want to buy her car from that dealer.

"I didn't like how much he was pressuring me," Samuelson said after we left. "He was kind of scuzzy."

To avoid that "scuzzy" feeling, Reed at Edmunds advocates doing most of your car shopping from home. Most dealerships sell their cars over the Internet as well, which can provide you with some advantages. Shopping online allows you to browse in the comfort of your home, away from the pressure tactics of a dealership's salesman. If you're nervous about your negotiating skills, or if you're a woman who's afraid a salesman will try to take advantage of you because of your gender, or if you're not confident in your language skills, shopping on the Internet removes many of those obstacles.

It allows you to compare the cars and prices at several different dealerships at once. It enables you to play different dealerships off each other. And perhaps best of all, it keeps you off the showroom floor, where it is easier to feel intimidated and overwhelmed.

"You don't think clearly when you're negotiating with pros," Reed said. "One way they manipulate the process is they know the process better than you."

Of course, you can't do everything virtually. No matter what, you're going to have some interaction with someone at the dealership, most likely the Internet manager on the phone. Make sure he knows you've been looking at what other dealerships are offering, and that you're fully aware of the Kelley Blue Book value, the incentives that are offered on the car, and the financing that's available. In fact, you can have them all up on your screen as you talk to him or her.

Before buying any car, either in person or over the Internet, you should always test-drive it first. And not just a car of the same make and model—the actual car itself. Don't just take it around the block. If possible, take it on the highway to see how it responds. Make sure the seats are comfortable and the features are exactly what you want. If you buy it, it likely will be your car for a long time. Make sure it's "the one."

Whether you're buying a car online or at the dealership, always ask what the "out-the-door" cost is. Essentially, that means the total amount you'll pay, including the sales tax, licensing fees, and documentation fees. Dealers often try to add "extras" to your contract to increase their profits, larding it up with shipping fees that are already covered in the price, and unnecessary add-ons like fabric treatments, rustproofing, or extended warranties.

"As soon as you ask what the out-the-door cost is going to be, they know what you're asking for," Reed said. "You're asking to smoke out any added fees."

If you're buying the vehicle over the Internet, ask for an e-mail spelling out the out-the-door cost before buying it. The last thing you want is to think you're about to buy a car, then get handed a contract that requires you to pay more than you expected. Believe me, I get e-mails from car buyers all the time saying they were quoted one price but wound up paying another. There are few things more disheartening.

Before you sign the contract, do two things. First, if the dealership has a service center, walk over and spend at least a few minutes speaking to customers there. After you buy the car, you probably won't have any more contact with the salesman, but you'll almost certainly have to deal with the service department. Ask people in the waiting room how the dealership has treated them. Have they honored the car's warranty? Do they charge reasonable rates? If a problem arises, does the dealership back its car?

If you're satisfied with the answers you receive, move on to the next important step: reading your contract carefully. I'm not talking about all the rip-your-eyes-out-its-so-boring small print that's standard on every contract. I'm talking primarily about the numbers—the total cost of the car, all the fees, the financing costs, and any other unforeseen "extra" charges you might not have anticipated.

Keep in mind that there are no "cooling off" periods after you buy a car. Once you sign the contract, it's yours. You cannot return it the next day or a few days later if you suddenly come down with buyer's remorse or feel that you somehow got screwed. While there are lemon laws in every state, the threshold is often difficult to reach. Most require a certain number of breakdowns during the first year. None allow you to return the car the next day.

DON'T GET ABUSED WHEN BUYING USED

Most of what I've told you so far applies to new cars. Things get even trickier when you're buying a used car. With a new car, you don't have to worry about how it was maintained before you bought it—it's fresh from the factory. With a used car, you have no idea what the previous owner did to it.

Some dealerships will offer "certified" used cars, meaning they've checked the car out and are willing to back it with a warranty. Generally, certified used cars are a safer bet—but you pay for the sense of security. No matter what, ask if the vehicle is still under warranty (either the original warranty or an extended plan), and, if so, how long the warranty lasts and what it covers.

While it's a good idea to test-drive a new car before buying it, test drives on used cars are absolutely imperative. In fact, some dealers will let you take the cars for hours or even overnight to give the car a thorough once-over. Before signing any contract on a used car, ask if you can insert a clause that allows you to take the car to a mechanic of your choice. Tell them that if your mechanic gives the car a clean bill of health, you'll buy it. It might cost you a little more (basically, the cost of a quick but thorough check by your mechanic), but it can save you a lot of heartache—and money—in the long run.

If you find a car you like, take some time to research what it's worth. As with a new car, you can input the make, model, year, and mileage into a number of websites, including kbb.com, Edmunds.com, autotrader.com, and the National Automobile Dealers Association website, nada.com. The numbers will vary slightly, but you'll get a general idea what the car is worth.

Don't be surprised if the sticker price on the vehicle is way above what the websites say it's worth. It's common practice to price the cars extremely high so the salesmen can make a grand show of slashing the price by thousands, making you feel like you're getting a great deal.

For instance, if you find an SUV with a $25,000 sticker price, the salesman might say, "Don't worry about it, I've been told I can give it to you for $21,000 just to get it off the lot. In fact, if you buy it today, I can give you a really good deal . . . $19,000."

Of course, the vehicle's only worth $19,000 anyway.

"That's just noise," Reed said. "That's just them doing their song and dance, and you just listen to them and enjoy it."

In other words, don't fall prey to their well-rehearsed routine. The only way to ensure you're getting a good deal is to do your research—and make sure they know you've done it.

KICKING THE TIRES

While companies like Carfax and AutoCheck can provide you with information about a vehicle's history, not every accident, nick, or scrape is always reported. Always examine the car or truck yourself. It might sound like a daunting task, but it can be quick and easy.

Barbara Terry, an automotive expert and off-road race car driver, suggests first checking the vehicle's oil, which should be honey colored. If you pull out the dipstick to find it's black or has the consistency of molasses, your personal warning light should start blinking. A car owner who doesn't change his or her oil regularly probably has let other things slide as well.

When you're done checking the oil, pull the transmission dipstick. If all is well, it will be a red, raspberry color. If it smells burnt or has metal flakes on it, run away.

You can also unscrew or unclamp the air filter. If it looks prehistoric and is covered in debris, be wary. The filter is designed to keep dirt from your engine. A filthy filter might have long since quit doing its job. (If you don't know where your air filter is, do an Internet search for "change air filter," and several excellent sites will pop up, including one from Edmunds.)

Finally, check to see if there is evidence the car has been repainted, often a sign the vehicle has been in an accident. Terry suggests running your finger along every door jamb, and along the edge of the hood and the fenders. If you feel a tape line, that's a pretty good indication a body shop has done work on the car.

If you're trading in your car to purchase a new one, check various sources to determine how much your car is worth, but be realistic about your vehicle's condition. Sometimes, when a dealer won't go down any further on the price of the car he or she is selling you, the trade-in will provide a little more wiggle room.

Even if it sounds like a good deal to trade in your car, look at the numbers carefully. Terry said dealerships make a killing on used cars—more than they do on new cars. In many cases, the dealership will try to get your trade-in for cheap.

"They're going to try to steal it from you," she said. "They're going to tell you it's worth nothing."

Terry said the dealership will take your old car, put in perhaps $500 worth of work reconditioning it, and then sell it for a huge profit—generally more than $6,000. Not a bad turnaround.

To avoid getting taken, Terry advises first trying to sell your old car on your own. You can use the money you earn toward the purchase of your new car, potentially saving you thousands.

MAINTENANCE AND REPAIRS

For the sake of argument, let's say you skillfully navigate the car-buying minefield without getting blown up and you actually drive home with a new (or new to you) car. Hey, it happens. Somehow, Americans have purchased enough vehicles to clog the turnpikes and highways from Maine to California, right?

Inevitably, your car or truck is going to need attention, whether it means taking the vehicle in for routine maintenance, a flat tire, or a new transmission. So how can you be sure you won't get screwed over by an evil mechanic?

If you're like me and you don't know the difference between a cage rotor and a catalytic converter, you appeal to a higher authority. For me, that meant going to one of the smartest people I know, my friend Emily Ziring.

Why do I trust her? Well, after she graduated from the

University of Pennsylvania, she got bored and, for reasons I've never fully understood, decided she wanted to become an auto mechanic. She was the only Ivy Leaguer—and one of only a handful of women—in her class at the Universal Technical Institute, a trade school for mechanics. Upon graduation from UTI (I know, the acronym is a tad unfortunate), she worked as a service consultant at an Audi dealership and then a Jaguar dealership. In other words, she knows her stuff.

Her first piece of advice to find a good mechanic? Ask around. Talk to friends and neighbors. Check for local shops that have good ratings on Angie's List or Yelp.com. Make sure the mechanic you choose is ASE certified, which means he or she has been given the stamp of approval by the National Institute for Automotive Service Excellence.

"That's like making sure your doctor is board certified," Ziring said.

Once you've found a mechanic you can trust, enter the auto shop's phone number in your cell phone or keep it on a piece of paper in your glove box. That way, if your car breaks down while you're driving around town, you don't have to panic, and you're not at the mercy of the first auto shop with an available tow truck.

Whichever mechanic you choose, keep him or her honest by checking the shop's rates. If you're going to be paying for a repair that requires an expensive part, ask how much your mechanic is going to charge, then shop around for a better deal. Ziring says that dealership service centers can charge up to a

200 percent markup on some parts. Before the repair takes place, ask if you can supply your own part.

"Sometimes they'll let you," Ziring said. "If they want your business, they'll work with you."

To find auto parts stores, do an Internet search or look through the yellow pages. Call several and see which sells the part for the least.

To determine how much your repair will cost, all auto shops and dealerships use the same formula: (book hours) X (the labor rate) + (parts). The book hours represent the standard time it takes for a specific repair. Since all mechanics consult the same "books" that determine the number of hours per repair, the book hours for a repair (say, replacing an alternator) will be the same no matter where you go. So Ziring suggests asking the mechanic for his or her labor rate. The labor rate, or how much a mechanic charges per hour, should be posted on the shop's wall. If you know the labor rate for several different mechanics, you can shop around for the best deal.

If you decide to take your vehicle to a dealership for service, keep in mind that the "service consultant" who works with you is basically another salesperson who is paid on commission. The more repairs they sell, the more money they make, a fact you should keep in mind if he or she tries to upsell you on a synthetic oil or a fluid flush or even a detailing.

If a mechanic does a diagnostic check and finds a problem, ask for specifics. Take good notes and do a little research. Ask another mechanic what it means, or look it up yourself on the Internet. Before agreeing to any repairs, have the mechanic show you exactly what is wrong—in person—and what he or she needs to do to fix it.

"They're going to be much less likely to lie to you if you're going to come in and see it," Ziring said.

If the mechanic conducts a diagnostic check, ask to have the diagnostic fee or labor waived if you allow him or her to continue with the repair. If you bring your car in because you're hearing a funny noise, ask the mechanic to ride with you while you drive. It can save hours of diagnostic costs. And always ask how quickly your car needs to be fixed, then watch the response. If they give you a quick, firm answer, it's more likely to be an urgent problem.

"If they're wishy-washy, the repair probably isn't totally necessary," Ziring said.

Perhaps most important, read your vehicle's owner's manual. Automotive technologies teacher Ryan Hoffmann said all manuals include a routine maintenance schedule, which can help you decide if a mechanic's suggested fix is legitimate or simply a scam.

For instance, if your mechanic wants to replace your vehicle's automatic transmission fluid, check to see what your owner's manual says. If the manufacturer recommends replacing it every 60,000 miles but your car only has 20,000 miles on it, you might wind up paying for a service you don't need. Hoffmann said some newer cars are built so that certain fluids never have to be changed, a fact that is clearly spelled out in the owner's manual. That doesn't stop some mechanics from telling you replacement is necessary.

"Unfortunately, a lot of consumers don't take the time to

look through that book," Hoffmann said. "If you spend two hours a night on YouTube looking at mindless videos, spend just an hour and then spend that other hour investigating something that will help you down the line."

The owner's manual can also tell you if you need to freak out when your "check engine" or "service engine soon" lights go off. When one of the lights goes off, it's rarely as dire as it seems, my friend Ziring said. In fact, your "service engine soon" light is likely preset to go off at a specific mileage.

"Just know what all that stuff means," she said. "Empower yourselves, people."

Sounds like good advice to me.

Oh, and Samuelson? She wound up doing a bit more car shopping that weekend, visiting two more dealerships. After a test-drive, she discovered she liked the Ford Fusion more than the Civic. Of course, she didn't let the Ford dealer know that. She wound up playing the Ford salesman against a Honda dealer.

In the end, she drove off in a brand new, snazzy red Ford Fusion. She even got $850 for her old Malibu, which broke down for good on the way to the dealership and had to be towed the final few miles.

Now that's some quality haggling.

TOOL TIME: KEEPING YOUR MECHANIC HONEST

How can you tell if your mechanic is trying to rip you off? On major repairs, always get a second opinion, and watch for the four "warning signs" listed below:

1. Too frequent scheduled maintenance. Some mechanics and dealership service centers will push you to get maintenance sooner than your vehicle needs it. Always read your owner's manual and stick to the schedule it lays out.

2. Fluid flushes. Again, check your owner's manual, which can tell you when each fluid needs to be flushed. A good question for your mechanic is: would you do this to your car?

3. The myth of the "upgrades." Mechanics and service centers sometimes try to get you to purchase fancy name-brand fluids or filters, synthetic oil, or nitrogen in tires. Avoid the temptation. In most cases, the lesser-known manufacturer will do just fine.

4. Suspension parts. If your mechanic says your suspension is kaput, get a second opinion. Often, your supposedly shot suspension has plenty of life left in it.

REMEMBER:

* Before you go car shopping, do your research. Determine what kind of car you're interested in, and what it should cost.

* Log on to www.kbb.com to find the Manufacturer's Suggested Retail Price, the invoice price, and the average amount the car has sold for.

* Go to Edmunds.com to check dealer incentives and if there is a dealer holdback.

* Check your credit report before going car shopping.
* Consider getting a loan approval from your bank before you visit dealerships.
* Crunch the numbers. Financing terms can be just as important as the price of the vehicle.
* Never tell a salesman how much you can afford to pay each month.
* Don't be intimidated or feel forced to make an immediate decision. There are plenty of options out there, and plenty of other dealerships willing to sell you a car.
* Consider buying your car over the Internet—or at least shopping around on the web before you go to the dealership.
* Always test-drive a car before buying it.
* Ask for the out-the-door cost to avoid last-minute "extras."
* Talk to people in the dealership's service area to see how they have been treated.
* If you decide to trade your car in, consider selling it on the Internet. Often, you'll make more money than you'll get for the trade-in.
* Read the contract carefully, especially the numbers. There is no "cooling-off period" in car buying.
* If you're buying a used car, ask if it is still under warranty.
* Research the car's value using several different websites.

* Check for signs the car has been well maintained.
* To find a good mechanic, ask around. Make sure the mechanic you choose is ASE certified.
* Keep the phone number for your mechanic in your cell phone and glove compartment.
* Ask how much the mechanic charges for parts, and whether you can bring in your own parts to save money.
* Check the mechanic's labor rate, or how much he or she charges per hour.
* Ask the mechanic to show you exactly what is wrong with your car, and what he or she needs to do to fix it.
* Always ask how imperative the repair is, and request your diagnostic fee be waived if you agree to the repair.
* If your car is making a funny sound, ask the mechanic to road test it with you. It can save hours of diagnostic testing.
* Read your owner's manual carefully. It can help you determine if a suggested repair is truly necessary.

14

LOTTO LETDOWN
Saying No to Nigerian Royalty and Other Scams

Rev. Dan Brandt likes to think he has a pretty good internal lie detector, but as a priest, he's also a trusting soul. So when an advertisement came across his church's fax machine offering three hundred screen-printed T-shirts for $2.75 a piece, Brandt thought he had stumbled into an amazing deal.

After all, he had been thinking about ordering shirts to give out to church volunteers and parishioners, but he'd always held off because he didn't have the money. At less than $3 a shirt, he could afford to order hundreds.

"I'd give them away like water at that price," Brandt reasoned.

He jotted down the address from the ad and cut a $1,225 check from the church's coffers.

The screen-printing company cashed the check within days, but the T-shirts never arrived. Brandt left repeated messages on the company's answering machine, none of which were returned. Several months later he called again, only to discover the phone had been disconnected.

"People try to prey on churches. Some people are geared toward that," Brandt told me. "I can smell them from a mile away. I have a sixth sense. I guess it failed me on this one."

I've got news for you, Father: you're not alone. The combustible combination of an ever-expanding Internet and tough economic times has summoned an unholy army of scam artists from their home in the primordial mud. How unscrupulous are they? Let's just put it this way: if they're willing to take $1,225 from Nativity of Our Lord Church, they'll certainly have no qualms scamming you for a few quick bucks.

Today's scammers are sneaky, conniving, smart, and opportunistic. And opportunity, it seems, is everywhere. In the old days, fraudsters had to knock on your door to sell you bogus goods. At least you had the opportunity to look them in the eye. Now they can call, fax, text, and e-mail. They can infiltrate your computer and steal your personal information. They'll rummage through your trash looking for sensitive documents, decode encrypted data, and say just about anything to separate you from your money.

"Scammers are cunning," said Audri Landford, codirector of Scambusters.org, a Boone, North Carolina–based website she founded more than a decade ago to educate consumers about the latest scams. "There are constantly more scams out there. Some of them are really stupid and some are very clever."

So how do you protect yourself? Well, for one thing, we can start with the old adage: "If it sounds too good to be true, it probably is." In fact, just get rid of the "probably" altogether.

Let's get a few things straight right off the bat: you haven't just won some foreign lottery. I know it sounded exciting, but you can just forget about that e-mail that promises you four million dollars, or British pounds, or Turkish lira, or whatever exotic currency the scam artist is trying to entice you with. The seemingly ever-present e-mail scam (I receive at least one such e-mail every day at work) claims you've just won an Internet lotto, usually in Europe or South America or some other far-away land. When you reply, the scam artist/fake lottery official will ask you to send in a deposit to secure your winnings. The only one who strikes it rich is the fake lottery official, who suddenly has your money. No reputable lottery or contest will ever ask you to send money up front.

The same is true for so-called "sweepstakes" companies, insidious businesses that prey on our sense of financial desperation. How do they work? Take, for example, Steven Jackson, whose eighty-six-year-old mother, Jane, lived in a nearby assisted-living facility.

Months earlier, Jane opened her mail and thought she had struck gold. Inside an enveloped marked "awards notification" was a letter that claimed she was on the verge of winning $3 million. All she had to do was fill out the attached claim form and send it back, along with a $20 check for "processing."

Jane sent the check, but it didn't buy her a jackpot. What she had purchased was a spot on a mailing list distributed to dozens of other phony sweepstakes companies, all of which promptly sent their own bogus awards letters. Soon, Jane was receiving up to ten letters a day promising her unfathomable riches. Jackson said his mother was convinced one of them would pay off, allowing her to set aside a nest egg for her children. She began making two piles—one for the letters that offered the biggest prizes, and another for the letters that offered something smaller, say a mere $1 million. Those she would throw away.

By the time Jackson figured out what was going on, his mother had sent the sweepstakes companies dozens of checks—for a total of almost $1,600 in "processing fees."

She hadn't won a penny.

"Her desire to better the life of her children was repeatedly taken advantage of," Jackson said. "They were playing on her dreams. They were giving her a false sense that she was doing something for her kids."

Nothing Jackson told his mother could convince her that the letters were fakes. They looked real. They arrived sporting bar codes with long, seemingly important number sequences along the bottom. They had impressive seals and embossed stamps that looked like the work of a professional notary. One said in bold letters "Congratulations to you!" from something called the "Achievement-of-Award Nomination Committee." It promised that Jackson's mom was about to win $7,385,621.00. Another, from a company called "Registered Data Analytics," sent a certificate promising a $2,450,900 payout. It was stamped "approved and registered," bore the signature of an "authorized officer," and included a grand foil seal.

"They're very clever," Jackson said. "They produce them in her name. It's spectacular stuff."

To put an end to the shenanigans, Jackson took over his mother's bank account, had all his mother's mail rerouted to his address, and sent cease-and-desist letters to more than thirty sweepstakes companies.

"I kept trying to tell her no one gives you $3 million

in the mail," he said. "Especially if they're asking you for money."

In fact, it's a pretty good practice to never, ever send money to a person, business, or organization you don't know.

DONATE WISELY

If someone asks for cash, you at least want to know who they are. That extends to charitable giving.

In the wake of every major disaster, there's an outpouring of donations to help the suffering. It happened after 9/11, Hurricane Katrina, the tsunami in Southeast Asia, and the earthquakes in Haiti and Japan. It's truly amazing and heartwarming to see how generous people can be, and how often we're willing to help our fellow man. But disasters also flush out society's bottom feeders—truly despicable scam artists who set up fake charities in an attempt to profit from this benevolence.

If you decide to donate after a tornado, earthquake, fire, or tsunami, make sure you're sending your money to a reputable charity. The Better Business Bureau compiles a list of legitimate charities, as does the nonprofit American Institute of Philanthropy, which runs the website charitywatch.org. To make sure the organization is truly a nonprofit entity, you can check its financial records on guidestar.org, which compiles a database of charitable groups' federal income tax returns. The returns, called 990 forms, show exactly how much a charity received and spent during the tax year, and how much executive officers made.

> There's a mountain of information on the Internet, so there's
> no reason to donate blindly. Before you cut a check, check out
> the organization.

These same principles apply to virtually any solicitation you receive. If you get a call or a letter or an e-mail from someone asking for your Social Security number, your credit card number, or access to your bank account, run a quick background check before committing to anything. Unless you're sure the business is legitimate and divulging this information is necessary, there is absolutely no reason for you to part with it.

In one popular scam, fraudsters send you an e-mail or a letter on IRS stationery, claiming there was a mistake on your most recent tax return and you owe more money. If you don't pay immediately, you'll be penalized severely. These scam artists are good. The letters and e-mails look exactly like ones that come directly from the IRS.

A good rule of thumb is that if any agency or business asks you for money unexpectedly, there's probably something fishy going on. Call the organization first and ask if you truly owe something. And by all means, never call using the number provided in the e-mail or letter. Find a phone number independently and place the call.

Sometimes, all it takes to check if a business is real is a five-second Google search. Just a few days before writing this, I received a message on my cell phone from "Mary" with the "award notification department" of some company I've never heard of. She said that an entry form I or a family member filled out at one of the company's events last year had been pulled, and my wife and I had won two free round-trip plane tickets to anywhere in the continental United States.

That wasn't all. I had also won a two-night stay at any Marriott hotel, a $50 gift certificate to either Olive Garden or Bahama Breeze restaurants, *and* $100 worth of free gas. The entire message took up more than two minutes on my voice mail. "Mary" was so peppy, I thought my ears might explode listening to her. She left a toll-free number for me to call to claim my "prize."

I jotted the number down and hung up. Despite the fact that I could desperately use an all-expenses-paid vacation (assuming I ordered Olive Garden's $6.95 all-you-can-eat soup, salad, and breadsticks combo for every meal), my internal fraud detector was blinking bright red. First of all, in her phone message, Mary never addressed me by name. If my name had truly been drawn in a raffle, wouldn't she know it?

Then there was the small fact that I hadn't entered any type of contest. And why in the name of Pete was she so insistent that I "call immediately." I mean, I'm the one who won, not her. Why was *she* so jazzed up? She sounded like a cheerleader on speed. Surely her crack team of contest employees had my address. Why wouldn't they send me something in writing?

So I Googled the phone number. Within milliseconds, scads of websites popped up with warnings that the offer was a scam. Turns out, I wasn't the only one whose name had been pulled in the supposed raffle—so had virtually every other cell phone owner in the greater Chicago area. Imagine that. There were literally hundreds of testimonials from folks who had received the exact same recording.

Under normal circumstances, I would have dropped it there. But since I'm writing this chapter on scams, I figured I owed it to myself to call Mary back immediately.

What had I truly won? I earned the opportunity to drive during rush hour to one of Chicago's northernmost suburbs so I could attend a two-hour sales pitch from a travel agency. The recording said I had no obligation to make a purchase—even if I said no to their spiel, I would still get my free plane tickets, the delicious Olive Garden meals, the night at the Marriott, and my three tanks of gas. Of course, there was also a chance I'd be brainwashed into spending thousands on a timeshare in Nicaragua.

This was not my first run-in with such sales offers. I once tried tracking a similar business down while working on a story for the *Chicago Tribune*. When I drove up to the nondescript suburban strip mall where the seminar was supposed to take place, I found an empty storefront. I've heard from plenty of readers who spent an evening of their time sitting through the sales pitch, only to learn that to redeem their "prize," they had to pay hundreds (and in some cases thousands) of dollars in taxes and fees.

I decided not to visit "Mary."

You might wonder how often these con artists succeed. The short answer: often enough to keep doing it.

You have probably heard of the seemingly omnipresent Nigerian Scam, which is basically a variation of the lottery scheme. In it, some member of royalty from a far-off land contacts you by mail or e-mail, saying he or she needs your help hiding some ungodly amount of money before a roving band of rebels seizes it. The letters are usually written in a charming mix of broken English and garbled grammar. They promise that if you help them deposit their $15 million in a U.S. bank account, you'll get a handsome reward, say 10 percent.

If you agree to help, the slow dance begins. After a short delay, the scam artist tells you the money has been tied up in customs, or is stuck in some foreign bank. The fraudster will ask you to send some small amount, say $1,000, to help scoot the process along. They're hoping that doesn't sound bad when you put it in context. After all, you're about to receive a $1.5 million windfall, right? You send the $1,000 only to find the transaction has hit another snag. Could you send another $3,000? And so it continues, until either your bank account is drained or you finally wise up.

"This is a $200-million-a-year scam, so obviously people are taken by it," Landford said. "Usually it's people who are fairly desperate for one reason or another—either they've recently gotten fired or they have some big medical expenses. They're more susceptible, so common sense goes out the window."

Even more devious is a similar scam, in which the fraudster actually sends you a check or money order and asks you to hold on to it for a few days. You're supposed to deposit the check into your banking account, wait for it to clear, take your cut, and wire the rest to a predetermined associate. If they've sent you $50,000, they'll tell you to take $5,000 for yourself and forward the remaining $45,000.

On the face of it, it sounds reasonable. After all, if the

check they've sent you clears your bank, what could possibly go wrong? Well, due to a quirk in the way banks process larger checks, the check can appear to have cleared while the bank continues to investigate its legitimacy. The full process can take weeks or even months in some cases. By the time your bank has determined the check you deposited was bogus, you've already wired the $45,000 from your savings account, leaving you on the hook for the full amount.

Again, if someone wants to give you money for doing little or no work, do not respond. There are no free meals in this world, and there are certainly no free cash windfalls.

What else can you do to reduce your exposure to scam artists? Install spyware on your computer and keep it updated. Educate yourself about the latest scams by checking with scambusters.org, your attorney general's website, or your local Better Business Bureau office.

If you have an e-mail account, install spam filters. If spam makes it through, erase those e-mails immediately, and by all means, never respond.

"Pretty much 100 percent of spam is scams," Landford said.

Don't do business with companies you don't know. It seems simple enough, but the allure of getting a fantastic price on a new camera or plasma television or custom-screened T-shirts can sometimes overwhelm your senses. If you find someone selling a product at a rock-bottom price, there's usually a reason. Do some research about whom you're buying from, or go with a well-known and trusted company.

Be vigilant. In one increasingly popular scam, someone calls you pretending to be from the local courthouse. The con artist says you recently missed jury duty. You say that's impossible. They respond, "Well, isn't this Jon Yates, Social Security number 444-55-6666?" The correct answer is simply "no," or to hang up immediately. But you'd be surprised how reflexive it is to respond, "No, my Social Security number is," and give your actual number.

I've said it before and I'll say it again, never, ever give out your personal or financial information unless you're dead certain whom you're giving it to.

This holds particularly true for senior citizens, who are by far the most frequent targets of scam artists. Why? For several reasons. Terence McElroy, a spokesman for the Florida Department of Agriculture and Consumer Services, says seniors generally have more assets than younger folks, making them more attractive to scammers. Some seniors are also widows or widowers, which means they don't have a spouse to bounce things off of.

McElroy also believes times have simply changed. Most seniors grew up in another era, one when you knew the people you did business with.

"It was a different time," McElroy said. "I know it sounds like an old cliché, but people didn't lock their doors at night and kids could run around unsupervised."

It sounds terrible, but in many parts of the country, those days are gone. So are the days when you could trust that people were on the up-and-up. Reserve your trust for the people, businesses, and organizations you know and respect.

There is no way I could list all of the scams that are out there. Even if I did, scam artists are constantly changing, so it's a good idea to check scam-fighting websites every few months, or to call your local attorney general's office and ask about the latest trends.

If you do get scammed, don't be embarrassed—scam artists have been honing their trade for eons. Fight back. File a police report with your local law enforcement agency, contact the Better Business Bureau, and share your story online at sites like www.scambusters.org. You might not get your money back, but you will help others avoid the bad guys. Don't forget, we're all in this together.

TRIANGLE OF TROUBLE

While the majority of scams outlined in this chapter involve fly-by-night shysters, one of the most popular and diabolical con games enlists your friends and relatives.

The simple and seductive pyramid scheme has been around for decades, and tends to flourish in tough economic times.

"They're epidemic right now," said Robert FitzPatrick, president of the Charlotte, North Carolina–based nonprofit Pyramid Scheme Alert. "These schemes have hijacked the American Dream."

The concept is straightforward. The most popular variety starts with one person who recruits two friends to pay him or her a fee, say $1,000. The two new recruits are instructed to each find two more participants, creating a new base of four people. Each pays another $1,000, which goes to the person at the top of the pyramid. The recruiting continues for one more round, until the person at the top walks away with $8,000.

Each participant then moves up a level, hoping to reach the top and get their own $8,000.

The problem, FitzPatrick said, is that the pyramid is unsustainable. At some point, there are no new friends, relatives, or neighbors to recruit, and the scheme collapses, leaving an exponentially large number of people at the bottom with no chance of making their $1,000 back.

"Nine people out of ten lose on such a scheme," FitzPatrick said.

Make no mistake, pyramid schemes are illegal.

The odds are even worse for multilevel marketing programs, or MLMs, which have exploded in recent years. Experts warn that some MLM programs are simply illegal pyramid schemes in disguise. Other MLMs are perfectly legal—but in most cases unprofitable.

In general, multilevel marketing requires you to recruit friends or family to help sell a product, such as herbal remedies or household goods. Because you get a commission on every sale completed by the people you have recruited, you're promised a big payout by simply finding new members.

It sounds like easy money, but it isn't.

FitzPatrick said that ninety-nine out of a hundred participants lose money, either by purchasing products they cannot resell, or by paying to participate, then finding no new recruits to join in.

"Pyramid schemes have become so pervasive, so ubiquitous, and so unregulated, they've become a part of our society," he said. "It's almost the new model of our economy."

So how do you avoid getting taken? The key, FitzPatrick said, is to avoid any program or club where the value of your investment is only realized when others come in behind you. If you have to recruit other members in order to make money, walk away.

REMEMBER:

* If it sounds too good to be true, it is.
* You have not won some foreign lottery.
* No legitimate contest or lottery will ask you to pay a "processing fee" to receive your winnings.
* If a business or company asks you for money out of the blue, do some research to find out if it is legit.
* Before you donate to a charity, check it out at Charitywatch.org, the Better Business Bureau, or on Guidestar.org.
* Never give out your Social Security number, credit card number, or bank account information to an unknown phone caller.
* Beware of Nigerian royalty—or anyone else—asking you to shelter large sums of money. You will not get your share. You will just get taken.
* If someone forwards you a check and asks you to keep a portion and forward the rest, rip it up. It's a scam.
* If you're recruited to join a club that requires you to pay money up front and recruit more members in order to recoup your investment, be wary. It's likely a pyramid scheme.

* Install spyware on your computer.
* Keep updated on the latest scams.
* Never respond to spam.
* Only do business with companies you know and trust.
* If you do get scammed, report it.

15

THE SILK-LINED COFFIN
Planning a Funeral without Being Exploited

Jayleen Castaneda's life was too short and entirely too painful. She suffered a pulmonary hemorrhage at birth and spent the first two weeks of her life on life support. As she struggled to survive, Jayleen developed bleeding on her brain, then a blood clot. She was only five months old when she died.

Her grief-stricken parents made it their mission to give her a proper grave site. They wanted a place they could visit on weekends to remember her. They picked a nice plot in a cemetery not far from their house. The section was reserved for children, so virtually every gravestone was adorned with bright flowers and colorful balloons, stuffed animals, and toys. For a place filled with acute sorrow, it exuded a certain happiness. It seemed like a place they could celebrate Jayleen's life, not mourn her death.

"Our first priority was to pay for her grave marker and place her pretty little face on it, because she was such an inspiration and a courageous and strong baby who fought so hard to live," said her mother, Aurora Castaneda.

After picking the plot, Castaneda and her husband drove to the monument company closest to the cemetery, a place called Hillside Memorials. It was literally across the street. The storefront looked nice, and the literature inside the shop said it had been around for decades. Everything about it seemed reputable.

They paid the monument company $1,700 up front for an elaborately etched headstone and were told it would be delivered in four to six weeks. The Castanedas visited Jayleen's unmarked grave every week, waiting for the headstone to be delivered. Six weeks came and went. Then six months. Repeated calls to the monument company were answered with a string of excuses.

After months of getting the runaround, it began to dawn on the couple that they had made a terrible mistake. Racked with grief and not thinking clearly, the Castanedas had gone on blind faith that the monument company was on the up-and-up. After all, who would take advantage of a family in its darkest hour?

The sad reality is that it happens far too often. Death is big business, and the funeral industry is just as riddled with scam artists and profiteers as any other trade. The National Funeral Directors Association says the average funeral costs $7,323—and that doesn't include the cost of a cemetery plot, a grave-stone, and burial services. In all, dealing with the death of a loved one can cost more than $10,000, making it one of the most expensive purchases most families will face, behind buying a house, a car, or perhaps a wedding.

So why do most of us put little to no research into the topic?

I know, it's not exactly the most uplifting subject matter. None of us like to think about a loved one—or ourselves—dying. But scrambling to make arrangements after someone close to you passes—when you're in a hurry and your judgment is clouded by grief—makes you a prime target for scams.

No doubt there are plenty of conscientious, fair, and compassionate funeral home directors out there. I'd wager that most of them are. The goal is to find them—and avoid the ones who simply want to take your money.

A little research can save you thousands of dollars and endless heartache.

Unfortunately the Castanedas had unknowingly stumbled upon one of the most notorious gravestone companies in Illinois. Just three years earlier, the state's attorney general had successfully sued the owner on behalf of eight people who said they paid for headstones that arrived late or not at all. A judge ruled that Hillside Memorials had engaged in "unfair and deceptive acts" and ordered it to pay the victims a total of $12,635.

Had the Castanedas taken a little more time and done a quick Google search, stories of the monument company's checkered past would have popped up immediately. In fact, I had just written about a similar issue with the company's owner, Caesar Rizzi, and Hillside Memorials months earlier. The Better Business Bureau had given the monument company an "F" rating, saying it failed to respond to ten of the thirteen complaints filed against it. But without any of that knowledge, the Castanedas wrote the $1,700 check, thinking a monument to their daughter was just a few weeks away.

Ed Markin, who runs the Funeral Help Program in Virginia Beach, Virginia, says funeral expenses vary widely, and that how much you pay depends almost entirely on the amount of research you do, and when you do it.

Markin says you can save about 50 percent by shopping around and getting written quotes before you need them. He suggests talking with your loved ones about what they actually want in their funeral—whether they want to be cremated or buried, the type of casket they want, and the type of memorial service they envision.

Markin believes funeral home directors often guilt families into paying more for expensive caskets and services by implying that anything less would be disrespectful to the recently deceased's memory. If you talk with loved ones ahead of time and know exactly what they want to happen after they die, you can confidently deflect such overtures.

"People are in denial about death right up until the bitter end," Markin said. "You delay talking about it at your own fiscal peril, is what it all boils down to."

By shopping around ahead of time, you can play funeral homes and monument companies against each other. Ask them to match or beat other companies' prices.

In some ways, it's a lot like car buying. Although funeral home directors will never tell you this, the markup on caskets, flowers, invitation cards, and other products can be astronomical.

"If you have someone dead, they have no reason to bargain with you," Markin said. "If you don't walk off once, you haven't gotten a good deal. Generally, you can save $1,000 by just walking off the parking lot."

Markin said he once asked about a dozen funeral homes in North Dallas how much they charge for a basic, no-frills cremation. All of the companies used the same crematorium, so the actual cost of the process was fixed. The funeral homes' prices ranged from $710 to $3,800, Markin said.

"What else can that be besides greed?" he asked. "You can pretty much shame anyone into spending a lot of money, money they a lot of times don't have."

As with buying a car, where you should never tell the salesman how much you can afford on a monthly payment, you should never tell a funeral home if you received a life insurance payout on your loved one. You'd be amazed how often a widow or widower has walked in clutching a $12,000 life insurance policy—and walked out with a $12,000 funeral.

To protect consumers, the Federal Trade Commission established the so-called Funeral Rule, which requires funeral directors to give you itemized prices in person or, if you ask for them, over the phone. That means that when you walk into a funeral home looking for a casket, the director must show you a list of all the caskets his or her company sells, along with prices and descriptions of each, before showing you any models.

Before buying a casket, you can ask for a copy of the list, then call other funeral homes and ask them to e-mail or fax you their lists. That way you can sit at home and compare the prices. And let each funeral director know you are shopping around. Competition is your best friend.

The Funeral Rule also says you have a right to buy individual goods and services. What does that mean? Well, in many cases, a funeral home will try to sell you "packaged" deals, with commonly selected goods and services. Those packages often include things you don't really want—and exclude other things you do. In most cases, it's better to buy everything à la carte.

That way you get exactly what you need without paying for extra services. (Some packages include memorial DVDs, floral "tributes," and flower vans. Sheesh.)

Just because you've settled on a funeral home to handle the burial does not mean you have to buy the casket there. Under the Funeral Rule, a funeral home is required to handle a casket that you purchased elsewhere. The funeral home also cannot charge you a fee for buying the casket somewhere else.

If you decide to have your loved one cremated, the funeral home must offer containers other than caskets. For a full list of provisions in the Funeral Rule, visit the Federal Trade Commission's website at www.ftc.gov.

KEEPING CREMATION COSTS DOWN

As the cost of funerals has risen over the years, so has the popularity of its low-cost alternative: cremation, which can cost as little as $1,000, far less than the average $7,000 price tag of a funeral.

"What's been happening is there's a whole paradigm shift in our industry," said Buddy Phaneuf, owner and president of the Cremation Society of New Hampshire. "Consumers are becoming very savvy."

Often, cremation societies provide a less expensive alternative to funeral homes, in part because they have less overhead. Companies specializing in cremation have no need for large, well-stocked showrooms or elaborately decorated offices.

"It is a much different look and feel," Phaneuf said. "It's more retail oriented."

But like any commodity, prices can vary widely. It's imperative to shop around. Many funeral homes and cremation societies post their cremation costs on their websites, making it easy to compare them.

"There is going to be a huge price difference with probably little or no difference in the quality of service," Paneuf said.

WHERE TO GO FOR HELP

Most states have their own laws and regulations about the funeral industry. If you're not sure where to find the rules in your state, contact the state agency that oversees funeral directors. All states except Colorado and Hawaii have a funeral regulatory board.

If you feel like a funeral home has taken advantage of you, you can file a complaint with the regulatory board. If you believe the funeral home has violated the federal Funeral Rule, you can file a complaint with the FTC. Wherever you file your complaint, send a copy to the funeral home to show you mean business. Sometimes merely filing a complaint is enough to convince the funeral home to correct things.

If you don't feel you're getting a good enough response from the state regulator or the FTC, you can also file a complaint with your state's attorney general's office, and with the Funeral Consumers Alliance, a nonprofit organization that advocates on behalf of consumers. Joshua Slocum, the agency's executive director, said his office fields thousands of complaints a year. While FCA can't help everyone, it does step in and try to mediate with a funeral home on particularly egregious cases. On other cases, it helps guide consumers to appropriate agencies or resources.

Like Markin, Slocum advises consumers to beware of funeral directors who try to "upsell" you to the priciest, most flashy goods.

"Anytime [a funeral director] talks to you about a 'traditional funeral,' make a mental strike through those words and replace them with 'my highest-priced funeral,'" Slocum said.

If a loved one has just died, "the funeral director is in full control of their mental faculties while you're not," he said. "They're not clergy. It's in their interest for you to spend a lot of money."

Don't be pressured into buying a mahogany casket with a hand-rubbed finish, or a "protective" casket, which costs more but, in fact, does little for your deceased Aunt Betty.

"The reality is no casket is going to keep the body from decomposing," Slocum said. "It just isn't going to happen. Nothing's going to stop that body from going back into the earth. Grandma's not going to be Sleeping Beauty."

Spending more on a casket doesn't mean you loved a relative more.

"It doesn't bring them more dignity," Slocum said. "It doesn't get them to the afterlife any faster."

HOW NOT TO PLAN AHEAD

Another thing to look out for is prepaying for a funeral. Experts say prepaid plans sound enticing but generally aren't worth the hassle. While funeral homes advertise the plans as a way for you to lock in funerals at today's prices, saving you the cost of inflation, such plans are often fraught with problems.

If you are thinking about buying such a plan, review the contract carefully and know exactly what you're buying. Where is your money being held? Who will manage it? Repeatedly in recent years, accounts holding prepaid funeral funds have gone under, leaving the folks who invested empty-handed. Make sure there's a provision in the contract that protects you if the firm goes out of business.

In other cases, your contract is bought up by another funeral home or chain. To use the money toward a funeral, you are told to go to the nearest participating mortuary. That's fine if the mortuary is close by. It's not so great if it's in another county or a neighboring state.

Ask the provider of the prepaid plan other questions as well. What happens if you move? Can you transfer the contract to another area? Are there fees if you cancel?

In other words, be careful.

"Prepaid plans are a terrible idea," Slocum said flatly. He advises putting your money in a certificate of deposit, a savings account, or a "pay on death" account at your bank. Make a trusted friend or relative the beneficiary of the account so that when you die, the money is available immediately and does not have to go through probate court.

If your loved one dies far from home (for example, if you live in Oregon and your grandmother dies in Florida), call a funeral home near where you intend to bury the body. Although it might sound complicated to transport a body across the country, funeral directors do it all the time.

The last thing you want to do is involve two funeral homes—one at home and another in the state where your relative died. By calling two funeral homes, you immediately double some of your costs and leave the two businesses scrapping for your money. Competition is good. Paying two funeral homes is quite the opposite.

Of course, all of this advice does not apply in all cases. Sometimes, death comes too fast and knocks us completely off our bearings. Such was the case with the Castaneda family. After Jayleen was born, they spent months at her hospital bedside, in a fog of disbelief. When she died, they were understandably unprepared.

In the end, it took the monument company almost a year—and a call from me, threatening bad publicity—to finish Jayleen's gravestone.

I was at the cemetery the day Jayleen's father, Jorge Castaneda, saw the stone for the first time. Standing at his daughter's grave site, his eyes filled with tears.

"I had to find the money to pay for that stone, because we wanted it fast," he told me.

Instead, the family was forced to endure an excruciating wait. What did they learn? First of all, never pay the entire cost of a good or service up front. With all $1,700 in hand, the monument company had little incentive to deliver the final product. Why would it? It had already been paid whether it finished the gravestone or not. As we learned when we were talking about contractors, paying a deposit is fine, but always hold back some of the final payment until the good or service is completed.

The Castanedas also learned about the importance of research, particularly when you're emotionally compromised. It's during the tough times that our BS detectors take a bit of a breather, and when stress compromises our normally active defense systems. Fight the urge to take the easiest route. It almost never pays off.

Remember, just because someone smiles, dresses sharply, talks smoothly, and has a nice-looking storefront, it doesn't mean they're not shysters. As they tell young reporters who are new on the job: if your mother tells you she loves you, check it out. It's pretty good advice for consumers, too. You never know where trouble lurks.

REMEMBER:

* Before paying a monument company for a gravestone, do a Google search to see if it's reputable.
* Just because a relative used a funeral home or a monument company in the past does not mean it's good. Always shop around.
* Never pay the entire cost of a headstone up front.

Paying a deposit is fine, but hold some money back as an incentive for completion.

* Ask your loved ones what kind of funeral they want.

* Shop around for caskets and other funeral services before you need them. Compare prices and obtain quotes.

* Federal law mandates funeral homes must give you a full price list of all its products and services.

* The Funeral Rule also says funeral homes must accept caskets from other stores.

* If you are going to cremate your loved one, the funeral home must offer a container other than a casket.

* If a loved one dies out of state, contact a local funeral home to transport the body. Never involve more than one funeral home.

* Be wary of prepaid plans. Make sure you read the contract carefully and understand what happens if the funeral home closes.

* More expensive doesn't always mean better. Some funeral homes charge more for goods and services to pay for nice furniture and chandeliers in their showroom.

* Packaged burial deals might sound good, but buying products and services à la carte often saves you more money in the end.

16

BECOMING YOUR OWN
PROBLEM SOLVER

My car was already sputtering as we pulled up to the red light on 14th Street in my hometown of Ames. This did not come as a surprise.

I had purchased the Datsun B210 GX from a family friend, who described the car as "hip" and "well maintained." In reality, it was the color of mud (except for the spots that were riddled with rust), and it often died for no apparent reason. But you get what you pay for, and I had bought the car for a song. I was seventeen and even an old clunker was better than having no wheels at all.

Unless, of course, you're at a busy intersection and the car suddenly stalls. As I think I've made abundantly clear, I have never been what anyone would term "mechanically inclined."

So I sat there, with my equally inept buddy Steve in the passenger seat, hoping desperately that nothing was really wrong. I turned the key and nothing happened. I waited thirty seconds and tried again. Nada. I threatened to take the car directly to the junkyard if it didn't magically hum to life. It didn't.

With that, I depleted my entire knowledge of how a car functions.

We were about to get out and push when a couple of elderly women in the car behind us walked up and signaled for me to open my window.

"What's the problem?" one of the women asked.

"I have no idea," I said.

"Pop the hood," she instructed.

At first I thought she was kidding. I stared at her blankly. I was convinced it had to be a practical joke. I looked around for a hidden camera. There was none.

I pegged her at eighty, perhaps a smidge older. She had thick glasses and shockingly white hair. Despite her soft features, she exuded a certain toughness. Perhaps it was her ever-so-slightly menacing tone when I gazed at her in utter disbelief.

"Pop the hood," she repeated with an edge.

Dumbfounded, I reached for the release and popped the hood. The old woman and her friend dispensed of the pleasantries and immediately disappeared under the hood. They quickly began poking and prodding among the doohickeys and whazzamagigs that make all cars run. I could hear the women tsk-tsking and speaking among themselves.

"Yes," one finally said. "Yes, that is it. Definitely."

I heard some mild tinkering, and one of the women made a motion with her hand. "Start 'er up."

I turned the key.

The car revved to life.

"Come out here," one of the women told us. "I want to show you what we did."

The octogenarians proceeded to tell us, in incredibly minute detail, exactly how they got my 1977 rust bucket running. It was simple, they said. A little twist here, tighten a hose there. You know, car stuff. But their roadside tutorial just sounded like mumbo jumbo to me. I nodded and promised I could handle it myself next time, even though I knew there was no chance. I thanked them profusely, but they seemed completely unmoved. I got the odd sense they had done this before.

As I got back into my car and they returned to theirs, one of the supergrandmas (perhaps they were great-grandmas?) offered me this advice: "You really should learn a thing or two about cars. There won't always be an old lady around to help you out."

No truer advice has ever been given. At some point, we all have to stick up for ourselves.

As I write this, I am preparing to celebrate my sixth anniversary as the *Chicago Tribune*'s Problem Solver. During that time, I've helped nearly one thousand people resolve disputes with companies, organizations, and governmental agencies, and I've read more than 40,000 letters and e-mails from readers who, in ways large and small, have been screwed over by The Man.

I've helped consumers recoup more than $1 million in erroneous charges, cut through hundreds of miles worth of red tape, and spurred companies to improve their customer service practices.

It's been a learning process, to say the least. My years as the Problem Solver have helped further my transformation from a short, shy, small-town geek to a no-nonsense consumer advocate.

I've picked up a fair bit of knowledge along the way, tips and insights that are spelled out in the pages of this book. It's a lot to digest. But if you take nothing else from these chapters, I hope you have embraced the basic concept: that winning a battle against a company or agency isn't always easy, but it's never impossible. It just takes some work.

Not everything in this book is applicable to everyday life. Some parts are specific to a certain industry or agency. Knowing the federal laws about air travel or the agencies that handle bank complaints won't necessarily help your fight against your insurance company.

But knowing how to find those laws and agencies just might.

Being your own Problem Solver doesn't have to take years of study. The reality is, there are basic tenets that can help you become a savvier consumer instantaneously. They are simple ideas that apply to almost any situation, on almost any day. I've boiled them down to a list of ten. I call them the Problem Solver Rules. They are the concepts I've embraced both in my job as a newspaper columnist and as a frenzied father of two.

If you do nothing else after reading this book (or if you read nothing else in this book), take a few minutes and resolve to abide by these simple consumer commandments:

1. Before giving even a penny to any business, corporation, or organization, do your research. Check it online. Ask friends and neighbors. Do business only with companies you know or who have passed your screening process. You've worked hard for your money. Protect it.

2. If a business or agency screws you over, complain. Never sit idly by and let a company take advantage of your. Raise a stink. Write a letter to the CEO, or send an e-mail to the board of directors. Make it clear that without a proper resolution, the company will spend more time and money dealing with you in the long run. As my dad would say, be a pill.

3. The more times you complain, the better your odds of winning become. There are plenty of great customer service agents out there. The more often you call, the more chances you have of finding one of them. Take copious notes, and get every promise in writing.

4. If the business doesn't respond to your onslaught of complaints, file a grievance with the appropriate agency. Throughout this book, I've listed state, federal, and nongovernmental agencies that will help you battle virtually any type of company. Going to war alone is noble, but fighting with a well-placed advocate on your side is even better—it's smart.

5. Read your monthly statements and all of your contracts religiously. Never enter into a financial agreement without knowing exactly what you're getting yourself into. Avoid long-term commitments and watch out for hefty cancellation fees. If you sign up for automatic deductions, read your bank statements frequently. If you go paperless and receive e-bills or statements, read them just as closely as you would if they came in the mail.

6. Keep all your paperwork. This includes receipts, contracts, and correspondence from disputes. Find a central

location in your house to keep all your documents, a place that's easily accessible in an emergency. In the appendix you'll find a rundown on how long to keep different types of paperwork. And buy a paper shredder. Trash cans are like playgrounds for identity thieves.

7. Right next to your stack of paperwork, keep a list of contractors and tradesmen you trust, such as mechanics, plumbers, electricians, and furnace repairmen. Do your homework before you need help, so you're not in a panic when something breaks down. On your computer, keep a list of websites you trust in your "favorites" tab so you can access them quickly.

8. Join the Do Not Call Registry, install spam filters on your e-mail, and put an end to junk mail. Instructions on how to do each can be found in the appendix. Our lives are busy enough. We don't need to be inundated by annoying calls, irritating e-mails, or endless copies of the Lands' End catalogue. Although the Men's Cotton Ranger Fatigue Pullover is nice. Especially in Expedition Green.

9. Never, ever, ever give out personal information, account numbers, your Social Security number, or other personal information over the phone to someone you don't know. The same holds true for e-mail correspondence or if you're entering the data onto a website. Protect your computer by installing spyware and antivirus software, keep abreast of the latest scams by monitoring Scambusters.org and other websites, and check your credit reports at least once a year.

10. Vote with your pocketbook. Never patronize a business that treats you poorly, and always threaten to leave if you're not happy with the response. If the company still refuses to help you, make good on your threat and leave. There are plenty of excellent businesses out there that will treat you with respect and listen to you when something goes wrong. Those companies are worthy of your money. Your most powerful tool as a consumer is your money. Wield that power wisely.

Of course, none of this information matters if you're not willing to use it. As I said in the first chapter, I'm all in favor of civility. Few things in life are more disarming than a simple smile or a kind word.

But if that doesn't work, sharpen your claws. The ten rules listed above are all predicated on you first abiding by the Problem Solver's Golden Rule: stick up for yourself. If a business, agency, or multinational corporation takes your hard-earned money and fails to deliver, do whatever it takes to get it back. Okay, there are limits. I don't advocate taking hostages or lobbing hand grenades. But if you're right, use every legal means at your disposal to right the wrong. It won't just help you; it will also help the next consumer down the line. Keeping businesses and organizations in line is all of our jobs. If you let them get away with bad service, they'll never change.

My mom was the living embodiment of this theory. She stood a mere 4 feet 11 inches tall, but what she lacked in stature, she more than made up for in tenacity. Born and raised in Detroit, she rarely took no for an answer. Oh, she could sweet-talk you and sometimes that worked. But when it didn't, she tried a slightly different tack. She became what can only be described as a woman possessed. Unlike my mild-mannered father, my mom could swear like a drunken sailor. And when she grabbed hold of a cause, she clamped down like the jaws of a enraged pit bull.

When I was seven years old, my older sister, Ann, desperately wanted to play Little League baseball. For years Ann had played baseball with the neighborhood boys in the elementary school field, and when it came time to sign up for sports one spring, she decided she wanted to join a team.

While I love my hometown dearly, Ames, Iowa, in the late 1970s wasn't exactly the most enlightened place. When my mom tried to sign up my sister for Little League, league officials politely handed her a sign-up sheet for the girls' softball league. For days, my mom fumed. Then she fought back.

Although she knew nothing about baseball, my mother signed up to coach a Little League team. She was assigned the Indians, making her the only female Little League coach in town. She then signed up my sister to play on her team. For months, my mom pored over coaching manuals and books on baseball, determined to prove the naysayers wrong and manage the Indians to a championship.

It didn't happen, but for my mom, the most important victory had nothing to do with the score. My sister played the whole season and wasn't half bad. My mom only lasted one year as a Little League coach, but the experience helped her launch a long career of proving naysayers wrong.

Sometimes, you just have to try.

It's not always easy. I've spent the past six years solving other people's problems, but there are still times I dread calling a company and acting the heavy. I've learned repeatedly that shyness gets you nowhere, and being meek will get you steam-rolled. If you don't speak up for yourself, no one will.

The words of the two grandmas who fixed my car more than twenty years ago still echo in my head. No, I did not follow through on my promise to learn about fixing cars. But I also haven't waited for kindly old women to fix all my problems.

Now if my car breaks down, I know who to call. I did my research and found a trusted mechanic. And I know what questions to ask him before he starts the repairs. And I have a pretty good idea how to avoid getting screwed.

Most important, if I do get screwed by a business, I know how to fight.

Now it's your turn.

APPENDIX

Addresses, Phone Numbers, Websites, and Other Extremely Necessary Resources

In the pages that follow, I provide information on how to access consumer help on the Internet, by phone, and through the mail.

In all cases, information was current at the time of this writing, but some names, numbers, and addresses might have recently changed.

1: DIAL H FOR HUMAN BEING

To find tips and numbers on how to reach a human being at hundreds of U.S. companies, go to GetHuman.com.

The Utility Reform Network, a San Francisco–based consumer watchdog group, offers a much smaller list of tips, along with phone numbers for many phone and wireless companies, at www.turn.org/article.php?id=447.

To find a phone number for a company's corporate office, try typing the name of the company and "corporate office phone number" into Google.

If you get through to an office's automated phone system that requires you to type in the first few letters of an employee's last name, try punching in the following names, which are the ten most common surnames in America:

764 for Smith
564 for Johnson
945 for Williams
566 for Jones
276 for Brown
328 for Davis
645 for Miller
945 for Wilson
666 (yikes!) for Moore
829 for Taylor

2: POISONED PEN

What you see below is a sample letter showing the key components, layout, and tone of a complaint letter to a major business or corporation. To find AT&T's chief executives, I Googled "AT&T chief executives," then wrote down the names and titles that I thought were pertinent. To find the address for AT&T's corporate headquarters, I visited the company's investor relations website. I also visited the websites of several local media to determine who else I should send my letter to.

To find the address and contact information for virtually any major business or corporation, go to ConsumerAction.gov, a federal website that keeps a list of hundreds of companies. Click on "where to file a complaint," and then "corporations," and an alphabetical list of major U.S. companies will appear.

Note, although I am an AT&T customer, the following letter is completely fabricated. I do receive my phone and Internet services from AT&T, but I have never had a problem with either.

SAMPLE LETTER

Jon Yates
435 N. Michigan Ave.
Chicago, IL 60611
312-555-3874
Acct. # 123-456-78910

Randall L. Stephenson
Chairman, Chief Executive Officer, and President, AT&T
208 S. Akard St.
Dallas, TX 75202

Mr. Stephenson,

I have been a loyal AT&T customer for more than a decade
and have always appreciated your company's commitment to
service. Despite competition for my telephone and Internet
business, I have remained with AT&T because it has always
treated me fairly and I've enjoyed your products.

I feel compelled to write you, however, because in recent
months I have encountered a series of uncharacteristic and
frustrating problems. On Jan. 12, my Internet and phone service
went out. I called AT&T's customer service number three times
over the next three days (reference numbers 06298, 99053, and
78112) and was told repeatedly the problem would be fixed.

On Jan. 15, a service technician (Jim, ID number 1152287)
arrived and attempted to fix the problem. He could not. Four
days later, on Jan. 19, another technician (Fred, ID number
2251198) spent three hours at my home but also could not
fix the problem. After two more weeks and three more
technicians, AT&T finally fixed the problem on Jan. 30.

On Jan. 31, customer service agent Rhonda (reference
number 2201898) promised to credit my bill for two months'

worth of service ($127.89) because I was without phone or
Internet service for eighteen days. It is now June 28, and my bill
has not been credited.

I have called customer service more than a dozen times
and I have been told repeatedly the credit will appear on my
next bill. I have received five monthly bills since Jan. 31, and
the credit has not appeared.

To resolve this problem, I would appreciate if AT&T
would credit my account the $127.89 immediately, or send me
a check for that amount. As I mentioned earlier, I have been
a loyal AT&T customer since 1997 and would like to remain
one. However, if this situation is not promptly resolved, I will
cancel my AT&T service and take my business to one of the
other phone and Internet companies that services my area.

If you need to reach me, you can e-mail me at jyates@
tribune.com, or call me at 312-555-3874. Thank you for your
time, and I look forward to your prompt response.

Jon Yates
Acct. # 123-456-78910
CC: Ann E. Meuleman, Senior Vice President and Secretary
James W. Callaway, Senior Vice President, Executive
    Operations
Catherine M. Coughlin, Senior Executive Vice President and
    Global Marketing Officer
Richard G. Lindner, Senior Executive Vice President and
    Chief Financial Officer
Mary Ann Ahern, NBC5 Chicago
Kristin Samuelson, "What's Your Problem?," *Chicago Tribune*

3: BRAVE NEW WORLD

There is an ever-growing array of Internet sites where you can go to complain about a company—or view others' complaints. Below I've listed the most popular sites, and generally how they're used.

The biggest, and probably best-known, consumer website remains the Better Business Bureau's site, at BBB.org. The site allows you to file a complaint and peruse complaints that others have submitted. Unlike most Internet complaint sites, the BBB will contact the company on your behalf and try to mediate a resolution. The mediation service is free, but results can vary. The BBB also rates companies based on the number of complaints each has received, and how well the company has responded. The website is an invaluable tool for consumers, who can use it for dispute resolution or as a research tool.

Another website that offers dispute resolution is Angie's List, at AngiesList.com. To access previously submitted complaints and use the site's mediation service, you must pay a membership fee. Monthly memberships start as little as $3.25, and yearly dues are generally less than $40. The site is particularly good for dealing with local companies or business people, such as contractors, plumbers, electricians, or doctors.

Perhaps the most comprehensive consumer complaint website can be found at Consumerist.com, which is overseen by the Consumers Union (which also publishes *Consumer Reports*). Consumerist.com posts consumer stories from other publications, writes its own stories based on consumer complaints, and keeps a thick archive of articles about companies and consumer issues. The website compiles contact information for executives at dozens of companies and provides tips on myriad consumer issues. It's an excellent source of up-to-the-minute consumer news, and a pretty good place to submit a complaint.

The San Francisco–based nonprofit Consumer Action has an excellent website at Consumer-Action.org, which provides updated consumer information on a wide range of topics. The website also allows you to file complaints against companies and agencies, and it runs a consumer hotline that dispenses free, nonlegal advice at 415-777-9635, or 213-624-8327.

Another good website, My3Cents.com, compiles complaints and consumer reviews about companies nationwide. Although it does not provide comprehensive advice like Consumerist.com, My3Cents.com is better organized and easier to search. Simply type in a company's name and see what others have written about it.

The website RipoffReport.com collects customer complaints and provides consumer tips. The complaint section allows other readers to chime in with their thoughts or experiences, and allows the company to lodge a rebuttal.

At ConsumerAffairs.com, you can file complaints, brush up on consumer news, and read the latest list of product recalls. The website is not as easy to navigate as those listed above, but does provide another outlet for consumers. The same goes for websites such as Complaints-Board.com, MeasuredUp.com, and the unfortunately named Pissed-Consumer.com.

4: A ROYAL PAIN

There are plenty or resources available to help you with your health insurance issue. Listed below are some of the best, with a brief synopsis of what each offers.

If you have a life-threatening or debilitating illness, the Patient Advocate Foundation, a nonprofit organization based in Hampton, Virginia, can provide assistance in your insurance battle. You can submit a request for help through the agency's website at www.patientadvocate.org/help.php, or write a letter to:

Patient Advocate Foundation
421 Butler Farm Road
Hampton, VA 23666

The organization can be reached by phone at 800-532-5274, or by fax at 757-873-8999. The foundation offers assistance to patients who are facing specific issues with their insurance company, their employer, job retention, and/or debt crisis matters related to their disease.

If you have a question pertaining to Medicare, including how to appeal a denied claim, you can seek help through the State Health Insurance Counseling and Assistance Programs, known as SHIPs. You can locate your state's SHIP office by logging on to to www.medicare.gov/contacts/staticpages/ships.aspx, then clicking on your state. I must warn you, however, that some states' SHIP programs are easier to navigate than others. For instance, if you click on Michigan's link, it takes you to an easy-to-navigate website for the Michigan Medicare/Medicaid Assistance Program. Similarly, the link for Arkansas takes you directly to the state's Senior Health Insurance Information Program. But in Louisiana, you're directed to the state's Department of Insurance, which then provides a link to its SHIP program. If you live in Illinois, you're directed to the state's Department of Financial and Professional Regulation, where I could find no link to its SHIP program.

If you have an issue with your self-insured or employer-sponsored health plan, you can seek help from your nearest Employee Benefits Security Administration office. You can find it by calling 866-444-3272 or by going to www.dol.gov/ebsa. The website also has links to information about your health insurance rights, as well as information about the Consolidated Omnibus Budget Reconciliation Act (known as COBRA), and other acts pertaining to children's health insurance and other issues. It is a virtual treasure trove of health insurance information. Particularly helpful is a page that describes your rights when filing a claim appeal, which can be found at www.dol.gov/ebsa/publications/filingbenefitsclaim.html.

If you have an issue with your individual or nonemployer-sponsored group health plan, you can file a complaint with your state's insurance commission. To find your state's commission, go to the

National Association of Insurance Commissioners website at NAIC. org. Some states are more aggressive than others in battling insurance companies on your behalf, but it never hurts to file a complaint with your state's department of insurance or commission. Sometimes, one call from your insurance commissioner's office is all it takes for an insurance company to correct a mistake, and in some states the commissioner has the authority to fine or punish an insurer if they wantonly disregard state law. It's always worth a shot.

For more tips on how to deal with health insurance issues, visit Families USA at FamiliesUSA.org, a Washington, D.C.–based nonprofit that advocates on behalf of health care consumers. The website includes links to updated information about health care issues, provides tips, and gives sample letters for claims appeals.

The Kaiser Family Foundation has a helpful, if somewhat dated, website to guide you through the process of appealing a denied claim. Visit www.kff.org/consumerguide/7350.cfm for tips and easy-to-understand descriptions of your health care rights.Some health insurance companies have appeal forms available on their websites that can be filled out and submitted, streamlining and simplifying the process. If your insurance company has such a form, fill it out. If not, pen your own appeal letter. Keep it as simple as possible.

Countless websites provide sample appeal letters, and some are better than others. If you do a Google search on the phrase "health insurance claim appeal letter," more than six million results pop up. There's a pretty good one at BankRate.com: just type in "health claim letter" in the search field.

I've included a sample appeal letter below. The level of detail you include in your letter will vary greatly based on the complexity of your health issue, but the sample letter should give you a general framework for writing an appeal.

Aug. 12, 2011
UnitedHealthcare Member Inquiry/Appeals
P.O. Box 30432
Salt Lake City, UT 84130-0432
RE: Jon Yates
Health Plan: 877-12258-02
Member ID: 764986334
Group number: 654912

To whom it may concern,

I am writing to appeal the UnitedHealthcare's denial of claim number 283412 for a blood work conducted by Dr. Tim Baron on July 21, 2011 at his office in Chicago. From your letter of denial dated Aug. 2, 2011, UnitedHealthcare states the blood test is an uncovered procedure under the terms of my health plan.

Please be advised that the blood work is listed as a covered procedure in the description of my company's plan (see attached copy of my plan, with relevant portions highlighted).

I have also attached a letter from Dr. Baron, in which he states the procedure was necessary to test for high cholesterol, which I am at risk for given my family history. My company's plan also covers all preventive care (see attached copy of my plan, with relevant portions highlighted). Please note that Dr. Baron considers the blood work a preventive measure.

I have also attached a copy of a study from the New England Journal of Medicine that states cholesterol tests for at-risk patients should be conducted annually. In addition, I have included a copy of my doctor's bill and my medical records related to the blood test.

I believe UnitedHealthcare did not have all of the relevant information when the claim was originally reviewed and denied.

Based on the information provided, I request you reconsider your denial and allow coverage for the procedure. If you have additional questions, please contact me at 312-444-1111 or Dr. Baron, at 312-555-0000.

Thank you for your consideration,
Jon Yates
444 N. Johnston Ave.
Chicago, IL 60655
773-555-2222 (home)
312-555-1111 (work)
312-555-7777 (cell)
Jonpyates1982@hotmail.com
CC: Dr. Tim Baron
Twelve pages of documents included

Finally, if you have the time and really want to research the issue, the American Medical Association has a very detailed and informative sixty-five-page report on medical claims and appeals that's written for doctors, but mostly presented in straightforward language. You can access it at www.ama-assn.org/ama1/pub/upload/mm/368/appeal-that-claim.pdf.

5: THE UNFRIENDLY SKIES

To file a complaint about an airline, go to the federal Department of Transportation's website at airconsumer.ost.dot.gov. For service complaints, you can click on a form that will allow you to file a complaint electronically. You can also call the DOT at 202-366-2220 to record a complaint. Someone from the DOT will then call you back during normal business hours.

You can also send in a complaint to the following address:

Aviation Consumer Protection Division, C-75
U.S. Department of Transportation
1200 New Jersey Ave, S.E.
Washington, D.C. 20590

The DOT suggests including the following information in your
   complaint:
Your name
Your address
A daytime phone number and e-mail address
The name of the airline or situation you are complaining about
The date of your flight
Your flight number if you know it
The origin and destination of the cities in your trip
And, of course, a description of your complaint

If you send a letter, the government suggests you include a copy of your airline ticket or itinerary, and copies of any correspondence you have already had with the company.

For a full list of the federal rules for overbooked flights from which you are bumped, and to find compensation rules for lost or damaged luggage, go to airconsumer.ost.dot.gov.

If your luggage is damaged during the screening process, you can file a claim with the Transportation Security Administration, by going to TSA.gov. At the time of this writing, there was no online submission form on the TSA website (it claims there will be one in the "near future"). Instead, the website allows you to download a claim form. Fill it out and fax it to 571-227-1904 or send it to:

TSA Claims Management Branch
601 South 12th Street - TSA 9
Arlington, VA 20598-6009

The TSA website warns that although some claims are resolved within sixty days, others require up to six months to fully investigate. The website also contains a list of contact phone numbers for TSA's lost and found department, including phone numbers for every major U.S. airport. That list can be found at www.tsa.gov/travelers/customer/editorial_1693.shtm.

You can also e-mail TSA at tsa-contactcenter@dhs.gov, or call the agency at 866-289-9673.

If you have a concern or complaint about airline or airport safety, you can contact the Federal Aviation Administration by calling 866-835-5322, or by visiting www.faa.gov/passengers/travel_problems/consumer_hotline. If you want to mail your complaint, send it to:

Federal Aviation Administration
Consumer Hotline, AOA-20
800 Independence Avenue, SW
Washington, DC 20591

To find contact information for major airlines like United, American, Southwest, Delta, U.S. Airways, Continental, and a handful of others, visit On Your Side, a consumer advocacy site, at http://onyoursi.de/wiki/category/airline. The website compiles publicly available information for the airlines, and often includes contact names, phone numbers, and e-mail addresses for customer service agent supervisors and employees a bit further up the food chain.

The website AirSafe.com provides tips on filing complaints about airlines, and offers to review your complaints and forward them to the appropriate federal agency. A companion website, FlightsGoneBad.com, features some of the complaints.

6: TOUGH LITTLE GUYS

To check out if a contractor is licensed to do business in your state, go to Contractors-License.org, which provides a rollover map of the United States. Click on your state, and the website will provide links to the regulatory agency to contact. You can also do a Google search with the name of your state and "contractor license lookup."

To do a background check on a contractor or tradesman, check out the Better Business Bureau, at BBB.org. The site will ask you to type in your zip code, which will then take you to your local BBB office's website. The BBB also offers free dispute resolution services.

You can also enter a business's name at Yelp.com, which provides anonymous customer reviews. Personally, I'm a bit wary of trusting any entry that has only a handful of reviews. But if the company has more than a dozen reviews posted, you can get a pretty good feel for the general quality of the work.

Generally more reliable are the reviews at AngiesList.com, a website that provides consumer tips, reviews, and dispute mediation. Again, Angie's List is not free, but it does not allow anonymous reviews, which improves the integrity of the information.

7: THE PEOPLE'S COURT

Several websites provide basic information by state for small claims courts. ConsumerAffairs.com provides a useful link called the "small claims guide" that includes links for small claims rules in all fifty states, along with tips and advice.

Legal information website Nolo.com offers a pretty comprehensive guide to small claims courts, available at www.nolo.com/legal-encyclopedia/small-claims-court. It even includes a link titled, "Can I sue a groomer who burned my dog's tail?" The short answer: yes.

The website FreeAdvice.com is particularly helpful. Visit http://

law.freeadvice.com/resources/smallclaimscourts.htm for links to the brochures for small claims courts in all fifty states, as well as the links to the courts in each state.

8: POWER STRUGGLE

To find the regulatory agency that oversees your state's utility companies, visit the websites for the National Association of Regulatory Utility Commissioners at NARUC.org. You'll find a page that contains a map of the United States. Click on your state and it will take you to a page that includes contact information for your utility commission, along with a link to the commission's website. You can also call the National Association of Regulatory Utility Commissioners at 202-898-2200, e-mail the organization at admin@naruc.org, or write to them at:

National Association of Regulatory Utility Commissioners
1101 Vermont Avenue, NW
Suite 200
Washington, DC 20005

To find other agencies that can help you in your utility battle, visit the National Association of State Utility Advocates at NASUCA.org. In many cases, you will be directed to the consumer division of your attorney general's office, or to a nonprofit watchdog group set up by your state to protect your interests. Often, these agencies will also provide tips and help for dealing with cable, phone, and cell phone companies.

You can reach NASUCA by phone at 301-589-6313, by e-mail at nasuca@nasuca.org, or by mail at:

National Association of State Utility Consumer Advocates
8380 Colesville Road, Suite 101
Silver Spring, MD 20910

To file a complaint about your phone company, cellular service provider, cable, or satellite television provider, or Internet service provider, go to the Federal Communication Commission's website at FCC.gov. The FCC allows you to file your complaint using its online form, or you can call its Consumer and Mediation Specialist team during regular business hours at 888-225-5322.

To file a complaint by mail, send it to:

Federal Communications Commission
Consumer & Governmental Affairs Bureau
ATTN: SLAM TEAM, Room CY A257
Consumer Complaints
445 12th Street, SW
Washington, DC 20554

9: UNCIVIL SERVANTS

For tips on how to deal with a bogus parking ticket, check out former parking ticket judge Haskell Nussbaum's website at BeatThatParkingTicket .com. If you live in New York, check out NewYorkParkingTicket.com.

To find contact information for your elected officials, go to USA. gov. It even has a form so you can contact the White House, and names, phone numbers, and e-mail addresses for local city council members. If you don't have access to the Internet, you can call 800-333-4636.

The government watchdog group Common Cause also has a search engine that enables you to find contact information for federal and state elected officials. To use it, go to CommonCause.org. You can then enter your address or view a list of politicians and their addresses, phone numbers, and e-mail addresses.

For contact information on how to file a complaint with virtually any federal agency, go to ConsumerAction.gov. There you'll find a list

of federal agencies and what they oversee, along with contact information for each agency. The list is amazingly comprehensive.

If you want to obtain information from a state or federal agency
through a Freedom of Information Act request (known as a FOIA), go
to the agency's website and see if it has a FOIA link. Many state, local,
and federal agencies have a person or office designated to process FOIA
requests. Some will allow you to fill out a form online. If you can't find
a link, call the agency and ask where—and to whom—your request
should be sent.

Several websites offer online FOIA request generators. The Stu-
dent Press Law Center offers an excellent FOIA generator at www.splc
.org/foiletter.asp. The Reporters Committee for Freedom of the Press
offers a good one as well, at www.rcfp.org/foialetter/index.php. That
site allows you to select a letter designated for either federal or local
agencies, and lets you tailor your letter to a specific state. Be as specific
as possible, describing exactly what records you seek. Try to keep the
request to one page, and if you know what document you seek, ask for
it by name (and date, if possible).

10: MONEY BUSINESS

To find the agency that regulates your bank, go to the Federal Financial Institutions Examination Council's website at FFIEC.gov, find its
"consumer help center," and find the name of your bank. You can conduct a similar search with the Federal Deposit Insurance Corporation
at FDIC.gov.

Once you figure out who regulates your bank, you can file a complaint with that agency. Listed below is the contact information for
each agency:

The Office of the Comptroller of the Currency regulates national
banks, including those with the word "national" or the initials

"N.A." in their names. The OCC has an incredibly useful and user-friendly website at HelpWithMyBank.gov. You can file a complaint using the agency's online form, or call the OCC at 800-613-6743. To mail a complaint, send it to:

Office of the Comptroller of the Currency
Customer Assistance Group
1301 McKinney Street, Suite 3450
Houston, TX 77010-9050

The Office of Thrift Supervision oversees federal savings and loans and federal savings banks. To file a complaint, go to www.ots.treas.gov, or call 800-842-6929. E-mails can be sent to consumer.complaints@ots.treas.gov. You can also send your complaint to:

Office of Thrift Supervision
1700 G Street, NW
Washington, DC 20552

The Board of Governors of the Federal Reserve regulates state-chartered banks and trust companies that belong to the Federal Reserve System. To file a complaint online, go to www.federalreserveconsumerhelp.gov/consumercomplaint.cfm. You can also call the Federal Reserve's consumer help line at 888-851-1920, fax a complaint to 877-888-2520, or send the complaint to:

Federal Reserve Consumer Help
PO Box 1200
Minneapolis, MN 55480

If your bank is state chartered but does not belong to the Federal Reserve System, you can file a complaint with either the Federal Deposit Insurance Corporation or your state bank regulator. To file a complaint with the FDIC online, go to https://www2.fdic.gov/starsmail/index.asp. You can also fax the complaint to 703-812-1020, or call 877-275-3342. To send a complaint, mail it to:

FDIC Consumer Response Center
2345 Grand Boulevard, Suite 100
Kansas City, MO 64108

If you want to file a complaint against a state-chartered bank with your state bank regulator, go to the Conference of State Bank Supervisors' website at CSBS.org, and find your way to "state banking commissioners." A page will then pop up with addresses, phone numbers, and links for regulators in all fifty states.

Credit unions, unfortunately, are a tad trickier. To file a complaint against a credit union, you must first determine if it's state or federally chartered. The National Credit Union Administration regulates federally chartered credit unions, which are credit unions with the word "federal" in their names, or any credit union in Delaware, South Dakota, Wyoming, or Washington, D.C. State regulators oversee all other credit unions.

If you're not sure if your credit union is state or federal, you can look up your credit union's charter number at the NCUA's website at www.ncua.gov/DataServices/FindCU.aspx. If the charter number is greater than 60,000, your credit union is state chartered. If the number is less than 60,000, your credit union is federally chartered.

To file a complaint against a state-chartered credit union, you can find the regulator by going to the National Association of State Credit Union Supervisors at NASCUS.org. Navigate your way to "state regulators," where you'll find a page with addresses, phone numbers, and web links for credit union regulators in forty-seven states (not Delaware, South Dakota, or Wyoming).

To file a complaint about a federally chartered credit union, go to NCUA.gov "consumer complaints." Once there, click on the link for "federal credit unions." That will take you to a page that allows you to click on the state you live in, so you can file a complaint with your regional NCUA office.

If you're having trouble navigating the labyrinth system of clicks, you can call the National Credit Union Administration at 800-827-9650, or write to:

NCUA
Federal Investigations
1755 Duke Street, Suite 6043
Alexandria, VA 22314-3428

11: CREDIT CRUNCH

To obtain a free copy of your credit report, go to www.annualcredit report.com, the credit report clearinghouse set up by the three major credit bureaus under federal law. I highly recommend using this site and not others, which often charge you for their services. You can also obtain a report by calling the service at 877-322-8228, or writing to:

Annual Credit Report Request Service
PO Box 105283
Atlanta, GA 30348-5283

Listed below is contact information for all three of the major credit bureaus. Each has an easily identifiable link on its home page to begin a dispute process.

Equifax Credit Information Services, Inc
PO Box 740241
Atlanta, GA 30374
800-685-1111
www.equifax.com

Experian
475 Anton Blvd.
Costa Mesa, CA 92626
888-397-3742
www.experian.com

TransUnion Consumer Solutions
PO Box 2000
Chester, PA 19022-2000
800-916-8800
www.transunion.com

To learn more about how your credit score is calculated, go to MyFICO.com. The website also has tips on how to improve your credit score, what's included in your credit report, and common facts and myths about credit scores. You can also reach MyFICO.com at 800-319-4433.

12: STOP, THIEF

Perhaps the most comprehensive identity theft website is provided by the Federal Trade Commission at FTC.gov. The agency provides tips on how to avoid identity theft, and what to do if your identity has been stolen. It also allows you to file a complaint with the FTC. You can also call the FTC's Identity Theft Hotline at 877-438-4338.

The San Diego–based nonprofit Identity Theft Resource Center runs an excellent website at IDTheftCenter.org, which provides tons of information about the topic. It also has links to identity theft resources in every state, including contact names, numbers, and addresses for state agencies where you can file a report or complaint. The site lists each state's identity-theft laws, the costs for placing a freeze on your credit report and, in some cases, where you can go for free legal help. The organization offers free victim assistance at 888-400-5530. You can also contact the center at 858-693-7935.

The National Fraud Information Center, part of the National Consumer League, runs Fraud.org, where you can file a complaint about telemarketing or Internet fraud. It then forwards your complaint to the appropriate law enforcement agency.

The website PrivacyRights.org provides tips on all manner of privacy issues, including practical tips on how to protect your privacy. Mari Frank's website, IdentityTheft.org, provides a list of tips on what to do if your identity is stolen, and includes things you can do to prevent problems.

If your Social Security card has been stolen, the Social Security Administration will replace it, but beware, it will only replace three cards in a year—and ten cards over your lifetime. To ensure the theft hasn't impacted your Social Security records, call the SSA at 800-772-1213 to make sure your income is being calculated correctly.

If your identity was stolen over the Internet, you can file a complaint with the Internet Crime Complaint Center, or IC3. The IC3 is a partnership between the FBI, that National White Collar Crime Center, and the Bureau of Justice Assistance. You can file a complaint of any type of cyber crime at IC3.gov. Investigators can then refer cases to the appropriate federal, state, or local law enforcement agency.

If your passport has been stolen, search for the "lost or stolen passports" section at the State Department's website, www.travel.state.gov. You can also call 877-487-2778, or write to:

U.S. Department of State
Passport Services
Consular Lost/Stolen Passport Section
1111 19th Street, NW, Suite 500
Washington, DC 20036

13. CAR TALK

The website Edmunds.com provides car reviews, prices, and tips. There you'll find whether a manufacturer is offering incentives on the vehicle you want to buy, and what the dealer holdback is, if any. Edmunds has also created its own statistics called the "True Market Value" and the "True Cost to Own," which purports to tell you how much it will cost to own your car over time.

Also helpful is Kelley Blue Book's website, at KBB.com. Like Edmunds, it provides prices and reviews for new and used cars—you can find both the invoice price and the Manufacturer Suggested Retail Price, or MSRP. Kelley Blue Book is particularly useful if you plan to sell or trade in your vehicle, with a user-friendly system for determining how much your car or truck is worth.

NadaGuides.com also offers a price guide, reviews, and information about the cost to own a vehicle. To cross-reference information on yet another site (never a bad idea), you can go to Cars.com. Cars.com also offers advice on how to find a good mechanic and other car repair advice.

There are a couple of websites that offer services that will check the history of a vehicle, including reported accidents, the title history, and whether a car or truck has sustained water damage. Autocheck.com offers vehicle history reports for about $30 per report, or thirty days of unlimited reports for about $45. Carfax.com offers a similar service for about $35 per report. Carfax also has a bulk-rate deal on multiple reports. To check your vehicle's history, or the history of a car or truck you are considering buying, you'll need to know the Vehicle Identification Number, or VIN. Remember, however, that not all accidents are reported to Carfax and Autocheck, so always get the car checked by a certified mechanic.

Several websites offer state-by-state information on lemon laws. Most are also hoping you'll sign up for legal services, but the links to state statutes are free. Sites such as CarLemon.com, LemonLawAmerica.com and Autopedia.com all have information about state and federal lemon laws. You can also go to ConsumerAffairs.com, which has a "lemon laws" link on its home page.

For advice on car repair issues, check out Barbara Terry's website at BarbaraTerry.com. You can peruse previous repair questions in her "Barbara's Q&A" section, or look up specific topics in her news articles. Another excellent source is CarTalk.com, the website for the popular NPR radio show "Car Talk." The site is not only entertaining, it's chock full of information about, well, cars.

14: LOTTO LETDOWN

For a comprehensive list of the latest scams, as well as tips and scam-related links, go to Scambusters.org, where you can also sign up for the organization's free newsletter.

The Federal Citizen Information Center also keeps a running list of ongoing scams at www.pueblo.gsa.gov/scamsdesc.htm, and the FBI tracks cyber scams at www.fbi.gov/cyberinvest/escams.htm. For the Better Business Bureau's list of new scams, go to www.bbb.org/us/consumer-tips-scams.

To keep up with the latest pyramid schemes and multilevel marketing operators, go to PyramidSchemeAlert.org. The website gives a synopsis of active and popular schemes.

To research a charitable organization, go to the American Institute of Philanthropy's website at CharityWatch.org. The site gives excellent tips on how to donate responsibly, and how to identify reputable charities. The nonprofit watchdog group can also be reached by phone at 773-529-2300, by e-mail at aipmail@charitywatch.org, or by mail at:

American Institute of Philanthropy
PO Box 578460
Chicago, IL 60657-8460

To search a nonprofit's 990 federal tax returns, go to Guidestar.org, which provides a comprehensive database of charitable organizations' Internal Revenue Service filings. To access the information, you must register, which is free and takes a few moments. After that, you will be able to search the tax records of virtually every charity in the United States.

15: THE SILK-LINED COFFIN

For a full list of the federal rules that govern funeral homes, go to the FTC's website at www.ftc.gov/bcp/menus/consumer/shop/funeral.shtm. To file a complaint with the Federal Trade Commission, go to www.ftc .gov/funerals. You can also call the FTC at 877-382-4357, or send your complaint to:

Federal Trade Commission
Consumer Response Center
600 Pennsylvania Ave. NW
Washington, DC 20580

To find the agency that regulates the funeral industry in your state, go to the website for the International Conference of Funeral Service Examining Boards at TheConferenceOnline.org, then click on "regulatory agencies." A list will appear of state funeral regulators, with addresses, phone numbers, and website links. You can call the ICFSEB at 479-442-7076.

You can also file a complaint with your state's attorney general's office, which usually has a consumer-protection division. To find contact information for your state's office, visit the National Association of Attorneys General at NAAG.org. NAAG's phone number is 202-326-6000.

For an excellent collection of funeral-related tips, information, and rules, visit the nonprofit Funeral Consumers Alliance at Funerals.org. The organization provides a good synopsis of both how and when to file a complaint against a funeral home. The website also contains advice about how to approach many facets of the funeral process. You can call the Funeral Consumers Alliance at 800-765-0107, or write to:

Funeral Consumers Alliance
33 Patchen Road
South Burlington, VT 05403

Another good source of funeral-related information is the Funeral Help Program, at Funeral-Help.org. You can call the program at 877-427-0220, send it an e-mail at fhp4@cox.net, or write to:

Funeral Help Program
1236 Ginger Crescent
Virginia Beach, VA 23453

16: BECOMING YOUR OWN PROBLEM SOLVER

So how long should you keep your bills, receipts, contracts, and other important documents?

Let's start with the obvious—the ones you should never, under any circumstance, throw away. That list includes:

Birth certificates
Social Security cards
Immunization records

Marriage licenses
Divorce records
Death certificates
Employment records
Military records

Also keep indefinitely all records of contributions to individual retirement accounts, particularly Roth accounts. These can be vital in proving you've already paid taxes.

Generally, these permanent documents—and many others that I will elaborate on below—should be kept in two places. The originals should be placed in a secure area like a safe or a safety deposit box. You should also keep a set of copies someplace more accessible, like a dedicated desk drawer.

What else should you keep? Hold on to receipts for major purchases, including appliances (also keep the manuals), televisions, jewelry, furniture, and computers. For cars, keep your title, loan information, service records, and warranty contract. For each of these, keep the records for as long as you own the item, or at the very least for as long as it is under warranty.

It's never a bad idea to take pictures of major items as well, quick snapshots that can be used for insurance purposes if something goes wrong. If you've got a digital camera, take five minutes to go around the house snapping quick photos of your flat-screen television, your new fridge—whatever you think is appropriate—and then upload them onto your computer. If you have an account with Snapfish, Shutterfly, Flickr, Photobucket or some other online photo storage service, keep the pictures there. That way, if you have to file a claim, you have proof of the condition.

Financial records can be a tad tricky. Most experts recommend keeping your tax returns for seven years. Why so long? The IRS has three years from your filing date to audit your return, but the time limit doubles to six years if the government suspects you have underreported your gross income by more than 25 percent.

The seven-year-rule also holds true for financial records that you'll need for tax purposes, such as stocks, bonds, and investment records, certificates of deposit, savings account information, relevant credit card statements, home improvement documents, real estate records, and 401(k) contributions.

If you've had contractors work on your house or repairmen fix your broken stove, keep receipts from the work for about ten years. That way, if something falls apart after the contractor has left, you have documents you can use in court if you have to file a lawsuit.

Keep life insurance policies for the life of the policy plus three years, car insurance policies for the life of your car, and home insurance for a least a decade after the policy year listed. Again, it's important to have two copies of each—and to store at least one copy in a place somewhere outside the insured area.

Utility bills are also a bit tricky. Chances are, you won't need them in the future, but as we saw in the case of Vito Grimaldi, utility companies are known to make mistakes. Check with the utility board in your state to see how long each utility company is required to keep your records on file. As I mentioned, it can vary from two years to more than six depending on the state. For most of you, that will be fine. If you live in a multiunit building in which your meter might be crossed and you're worried you might be overpaying, keep copies of your bills indefinitely. It certainly helped Grimaldi.

For more mundane records and receipts, you can purge more often. As we saw in the chapter on identity theft, you have sixty days to file a claim with your credit card company if someone has used your account number fraudulently, so it's best to keep credit card bills for at least two months. Some experts recommend keeping your statements another month, in case you need to provide proof of payment on an item from a business or organization.

You can keep your pay stubs for the year in case you have a dispute with your employer, but there's no reason to hold on to them after that. Once your annual W-2 tax form arrives, check it to make sure your pay was recorded correctly, then shred the pay stubs.

For ATM deposits and withdrawals, you can toss the receipts in several days or at most several weeks, after you see proof that the transaction cleared.

The same holds true for grocery store trips and other small purchases. Once it becomes apparent you're not going to return your strawberries from Albertsons or the Radio Flyer wagon you bought at Toys "R" Us, toss the receipt. It's just clutter.

Okay, now that I've added clutter to your life, let's balance things out a bit by removing some of it.

If you haven't joined the National Do Not Call Registry, do it now. It takes only seconds, and can cut down dramatically on the number of telemarketing calls you receive. To sign up online, visit DoNotCall .gov and click on "register a phone number." You can type in up to three phone numbers, including those for your home and cell phones. You can also sign up by calling 888-382-1222. The registry is run by the Federal Trade Commission, which also handles complaints against companies that violate the Do Not Call law.

Now let's move on to your mail. Take few moments to visit the website for the Direct Marketing Association, DMAchoice.org. The organization represents hundreds of businesses and companies that try to sell you things on the phone, through e-mail and, most important, through snail mail.

Once on the website, you'll be asked to set up an account with your e-mail address and a password. After you've signed up, you can begin notifying the companies that you want to stop sending you junk mail. You can select the companies individually or do as I did—eliminate them all.

There's a link to halt credit card offers, another link to stop catalogs, a third for magazine offers, and a fourth, catchall category called "all other mail offers." Informing DMA that you don't want to be bothered at home does not eliminate all your junk mail. If you've done business with a company in the past, you'll have to contact it directly to halt its catalogs or mail offers from arriving. Still, spending just a few minutes on the DMA website can help eliminate virtually all of your junk mail.

INDEX